INTERDISCIPLINARY
UNITS AND PROJECTS
FOR
THEMATIC
INSTRUCTION

by Imogene Forte and Sandra Schurr

Incentive Publications, Inc.
Nashville, Tennessee

Illustrated by Marta Drayton
Cover by Marta Drayton and Joe Shibley
Edited by Leslie Britt

ISBN 0-86530-243-X

PRINTED IN THE UNITED STATES OF AMERICA

Table of Contents

Learning Centers

Read/Relate

Appendix

Preface

The Information Age has made a significant impact on the development of curriculum and on the delivery of instruction at the middle level. The "knowledge explosion" has caused teachers and curriculum supervisors to openly question both what is taught and the methods used to teach it. With the rate of information doubling every 2½ years in most disciplines, educators find themselves constantly asking questions such as "What knowledge is of most worth?" and "How can we present this knowledge in a timely and efficient manner?" Furthermore, educators are becoming more convinced that they must re-conceptualize their roles in the schooling process if students are going to be ready for the demands of the 21st century. Finally, it is important to acknowledge the research findings which clearly support the premise that early adolescents learn best when:

- teachers help them make connections among seemingly unrelated subject areas;
- teachers help them infuse processing and thinking skills into classroom assignments;
- teachers help them identify individual learning styles in order to capitalize on personal thoughts;
- teachers help them plan and create student products as evidence that learning has taken place;
- teachers help them internalize themes as a vehicle for organizing information; and
- teachers help them value the long-term benefits of interdisciplinary instruction.

Interdisciplinary Units and Projects for Thematic Instruction was conceived and written with all of these principles in mind. It was designed to make classroom instruction easier to deliver as a dynamic integrated and academically-sequenced whole and to meet both the educational and social needs of middle grade students. The interdisciplinary approach with a thematic focus has been utilized throughout the units and projects to stimulate multi-level thinking, to accommodate a variety of learning styles, and to create and maintain high interest in and zest for learning.

Within this framework the middle grades instructor will find hundreds of interdisciplinary learning tasks and activities organized under four major instructional delivery systems.

Major Interdisciplinary Thematic Units

- Twelve major units are based on high-interest topics.
- Each unit contains important teacher information (including the unit's purpose, content focus, specific objectives, and assessment), a glossary of relevant terms, content-based activities, and a journal activity intended to help students internalize the unit's concepts.

Mini Interdisciplinary Thematic Units

- Thirty-six mini units are based on Bloom's Taxonomy of Cognitive Development and Williams' Taxonomy of Divergent Thinking and Feeling.

Learning Centers

- Twelve learning centers each employ a unique format to capture and hold student interest: Pocket Packet (a set of ready-to-use task cards which can be stored in 5" x 8" envelopes), File Folder (reproducible activity pages ready to be mounted on a regular-size file folder), Portable Desk Top (reproducible activity pages to be pasted on a three-sided display board), and Investigation Cards (a set of task cards based on Bloom's Taxonomy ready to be cut apart and mounted on pieces of construction paper).

Read and Relate

- Twenty-four read and relate activities require students to read and digest information on a high-interest theme and complete a task that will help them internalize the topic at hand.

Additional support for interdisciplinary thematic instruction is provided in the practical and user-friendly appendix which contains:

- a special section dedicated to accommodation of differing learning styles, including a ready-to-use independent study project, a structured learning center, a mini unit, and a free choice interest center,
- an organizational chart for multi-grade grouping,
- an annotated bibliography, and
- a comprehensive index of subjects.

MAJOR INTERDISCIPLINARY THEMATIC UNITS

A Picture Is Worth A Thousand Words

— UNIT OVERVIEW —

Theme

Communication

Purpose

To provide students with an opportunity to explore the exciting world of photography as both an art form and a hobby. Cameras come in every size, shape, and price range today, and can be used successfully with any age group. Likewise, camera buffs can be found in any community or setting.

Content Focus

Language Arts

Assessment

Each student will use the camera to plan and create a photo essay, story, or comprehensive display on a theme of his or her choice.

Specific Objectives

NOTES

1. The student will develop a working vocabulary of common terms associated with photography.
2. The student will apply the basic principles for operating a camera.
3. The student will interact with a professional photographer.
4. The student will explore careers in the field of photography.
5. The student will construct a photo essay, story, or exhibit.

A Picture Is Worth A Thousand Words

── GLOSSARY ──

Exposure
the act of exposing sensitized photographic film or plate

Film Cartridge
a case with photographic film that can be loaded directly into a camera

Filter
material that transmits some colors of light and blocks others

Focus
the distinctness or clarity with which an optical system renders an image; a point in an optical system to which rays converge or from which they appear to diverge, that is, the focal point

Lens
a carefully ground or molded piece of glass, plastic, or other transparent material with opposite surfaces either or both of which are curved, by means of which light rays are refracted to form an image

Print
a photographic image transferred to paper or a similar surface, usually from a negative

Shutter
a mechanical device that opens and shuts the lens aperture of a camera to expose a plate or film

Tripod
a three-legged stand for supporting a camera

A Picture Is Worth A Thousand Words

Language Arts: READING

Locate a book about photography or a book of photographs in the school or community library. Write a short book review of its contents.

Language Arts: WRITING

Pretend you are a famous photographer who specializes in taking pictures of nature, of local events, of historic monuments, of beautiful buildings, of famous people, or of architectural wonders. Write a series of diary entries telling about your travels and photography experiences.

Study Skills: RESEARCH

Choose a topic or theme of special interest to you. Use reference materials to collect information about the theme to use to create a photo essay, story, or exhibit.

A Picture Is Worth A Thousand Words

CONTENT-BASED ACTIVITIES

Social Studies

Invite a professional photographer to come to your class or plan a field trip to a photography studio. Prepare a list of interview questions to ask the visiting photographer or develop a checklist of things you want to see and do during a visit to a photographer's place of business.

Math

Visit a camera store or use a catalog to compare and contrast any three different types and/or brands of cameras. Share your finds in graph form.

Art

Browse through magazines and newspapers to collect photographs of interesting subjects. Arrange these in collage form and use the completed collage as a springboard for writing a free verse poem about it.

Creative Thinking

Create a clever business card for a photographer. Name the business and design a slogan, logo, and unusual format for the card.

A Picture Is Worth
A Thousand Words

CONTENT-BASED ACTIVITIES

Optional Extension

Use a camera to do several interesting and unusual things such as:

- Take pictures of small objects up close or large objects from far away.
- Take pictures from unusual angles.
- Take pictures of unique people, places, or things.
- Take pictures through glass.
- Take candid pictures of people who do not pose or who do not know that you are taking their pictures.
- Take pictures of objects that are moving.

Arrange a time for projects to be displayed and discussed.

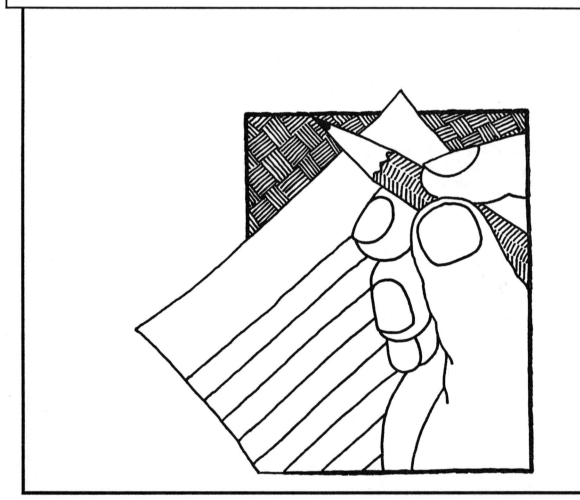

A Picture Is Worth A Thousand Words

JOURNALING

Paste a recent photograph of yourself here. Look carefully at the photo, then write about the image the photo portrays. Do you see a smiling, happy face, a grumpy quarrelsome face, or perhaps a hard-to-read face? Did the photographer capture the real you? Tell how this photograph agrees with and/or disagrees with the "real" you as you would like your friends to perceive you. Respond in a journal entry to any, all, or none of these questions as you write about "The Real Me."

_____

_____

_____

_____

_____

_____

_____

_____

_____

_____

_____

_____

_____

_____

_____

_____

_____

_____

_____

_____

_____

_____

Unplugging The Television Set

Theme

Communication

Purpose

To make students more aware of their television viewing habits as well as to examine the types of programs that are most popular with the viewing audience. Students will also have an opportunity to analyze the types and elements of typical television shows as well as the influences of advertising techniques on commercials.

Content Focus

Social Studies

Assessment

The student will maintain a folder of his or her television activity results and will both create an original television commercial and participate in an original television classroom production.

Specific Objectives

NOTES

1. The student will uncover his or her favorite types of television programs and preferred times for watching these programs.
2. The student will identify the various types of television programs being aired today and the general appeal of each type.
3. The student will explore reasons why television is a popular pastime with both kids and adults.
4. The student will describe the key elements of a television adventure, drama, comedy, crime, or science fiction show.
5. The student will demonstrate an understanding of how television contributes to stereotyping of people and their personalities and/or work roles.
6. The student will experiment with the effects of camera angles on objects.
7. The student will identify various advertising strategies used in television commercials.
8. The student will help to plan and produce a television show.
9. The student will analyze the effectiveness of various anchors on local and national television news shows.

Unplugging The Television Set

GLOSSARY

Anchor
the person who explains and coordinates coverage which is given by one or more reporters

Close-up
the kind of camera shot which makes the object or person seem very close to you

Commercials
advertisements on TV which help pay for the TV programs

Director
the person who is in charge of making a TV program by deciding how actors should act, which props to use, and which cameras to use

Documentary
close look at a special subject which presents all sides to an issue

News Program
a show that features information from our own community and around the world

Prejudice
to judge people or situations before you know about them, or to already have ideas about them

Prime-Time
the part of the television schedule between eight and eleven o'clock in the evening which is watched by the most people and which carries the most expensive commercials

Producer
the person who creates and organizes TV programs and who handles the production budget

Script
the written text of both the picture and sound parts of a TV program

Set
different pieces of painted scenery and props used in a TV studio to create a certain mood for the designated program

Shot
each picture that the camera takes

Sponsor
a person, business, or group that helps pay for the cost of a TV program so that it can advertise its product during the broadcast

Stereotype
the oversimplified ideas we have when we apply the characteristics of an individual to an entire group

Zoom
a lens that can make an object or person appear very close or very far away without moving the camera

Unplugging The Television Set

CONTENT-BASED ACTIVITIES

Social Studies: SELF-AWARENESS

Maintain a weekly log of your television viewing habits. For each day of the week, record the names of all television shows that you watch, the channel on which each show is found, the time that each program is shown, and a brief reaction to the theme of each show. Organize this information into a chart and draw some conclusions about your viewing habits by completing the starter statement: "From my TV viewing log I learned that . . ."

Math

Browse through your local TV guide and write down the name of a popular show for each of the following program categories:

- Dramas
- Cartoons
- Talk Shows
- Game Shows
- Variety Shows
- Documentaries
- News Programs
- Sports Programs
- Crime or Detective Shows
- Educational Programs
- Serials or Soap Operas
- Comedy Series Programs
- Adventure Shows
- Science Fiction or Fantasy Shows

Choose a day during the week to calculate the number of shows for each program category and record your results in a large pie or circle graph.

Study Skills: RESEARCH

Design a simple research study to determine the most common reason(s) people watch television during their leisure time. Consider such reasons as:

- for information
- for entertainment
- for adventure
- for an assignment
- for something to do
- for relaxation
- for change of pace
- to relieve boredom
- because it is there
- because friends and family do it

Conduct additional research to find out as much as you can about national television viewing habits. Prepare an information brochure that tells people about the facts and dangers of watching too much television and that provides the reader with suggestions for reducing the amount of time watching television and for other ways to spend their leisure time at home.

Unplugging The Television Set

CONTENT-BASED ACTIVITIES

Language Arts: WRITING

Choose a favorite situation comedy, drama, adventure, crime, or science fiction show to watch. Write a simple review of the show, describing each of the following program elements:

• CHARACTERS: List the major characters in the show. Tell how they look, act, speak, and feel about one another.
• SETTING: Describe the basic setting of the show. Discuss the time of year and day the action is taking place as well as how the setting helps create the mood or feeling of the story.
• CONFLICT: Summarize the problem, argument, or disagreement that is causing a conflict between the major characters. Tell how the conflict is resolved.
• PLOT: Explain three major events in the order that they happened in the story.
• THEME: Write a sentence that states the primary message or purpose of the story.
• LOGIC: Determine what parts of the story could really happen and what parts of the story seem unlikely to happen in real-life situations.

Social Studies

Television often promotes false impressions of specific people and their roles or personalities. These are called stereotypes. Think about all the television programs, especially situation comedies and crime shows, that you watch. If you were a visitor from outer space and the only information you had about Americans was what you observed from watching television, what false impressions might you develop about life in the United States? Write your ideas in a short essay.

Science

Television cameras can make the characters and events that they photograph appear in interesting ways. Draw a picture of a tree and show it from the following camera angles:

• A long-shot view that shows the full length of the tree and much of its surroundings
• A close-up view that shows the only a part of the tree and very little of its surroundings
• A tilted-up view that shows the tree from the ground up
• A tilted-down view that shows the tree from very high up

Unplugging The Television Set

CONTENT-BASED ACTIVITIES

Creative Thinking

Describe the details of your favorite television commercial and give reasons why you find it effective. Consider these common advertising techniques used to enhance television commercials: close-up shots of people, places, or things; sound effects; special lighting; use of music or songs; happy settings; humor; and endorsements by attractive people or celebrities. Create an original television commercial advertising an imaginary product. Incorporate as many of these advertising techniques as you can.

Enrichment: DRAMA

Work with the students in your class to plan and produce an original television show. Decide on the following job roles and responsibilities before you begin the production process.

- Casting Director to find the best people to act in the show
- Actors and Actresses to perform the show's script
- Set Designer to develop and oversee the building of the sets
- Costume Designer to draw costume designs and see that they are obtained for the actors and actresses
- Music Coordinator to select and direct background music
- Make-up Artist to apply make-up
- Audio Engineer to create and direct sound effects
- Cameraman to handle video camera
- Lighting Designer to arrange for lighting effects
- Script Writers who create the script
- Producer to develop a production budget and obtain funding
- Commentator to introduce show and handle station breaks

Use the original commercials from the Creative Thinking activity for advertising with your television program.

Optional Extension

View several daily news shows and make a list of the most common news personalities. Decide what characteristics you feel are important for a news anchor to have and write these down. Create a rating scale from 1 to 10. Develop a line graph figure similar to the one shown that compares the news personalities with one another. Put the characteristics to be rated along the horizontal axis and the rating scale along the vertical axis. Provide a color scale assigning a different color to each person and connect the points on the scale to give you a summary of your results.

Characteristics To Be Rated			
10			
9			
8			
7			
6			
5			
4			
3			
2			
1			
0			

Unplugging The Television Set

— JOURNALING —

Respond in a journal entry to one or more of the following questions.
- What would you do if TV were forbidden in your home for a year?
- If you could receive a meaningful reward for giving your television set away, what would you want? Explain why.
- If your TV set were sold at an auction for homeless people, what special gifts would you give each member of your family for consolation or for replacement? Explain the significance of each gift.

Writing About Me, Myself, And I

─── UNIT OVERVIEW ───

Theme

Communication

Purpose

To use one's personal self as the springboard for a variety of communication skill activities including reading, writing, listening, and speaking. Each activity is designed to be self-reflective in some way and is intended to help the student look at his or her strengths from a variety of perspectives.

Content Focus

Language Arts

Assessment

The student will compile a portfolio of artifacts whose theme reflects his or her personal interests, experiences, wishes, perceptions, and school events.

Specific Objectives

NOTES

1. The student will construct an "ABC Book" of his or her favorite people, places, or things.
2. The student will prepare a persuasive piece of writing on a topic of emotional importance to him or her.
3. The student will draw a set of original illustrations to reflect memorable moments in his or her life to date.
4. The student will construct an "Excitement Level Graph" to analyze his or her passion for topics currently being taught at school.
5. The student will design an advertising piece in support of an environmental cause.
6. The student will engage in a series of original writing tasks.
7. The student will compile a "Book of Lists" to summarize information about him- or herself.

Writing About Me, Myself, And I

GLOSSARY

Autobiography
the biography of a person written by him- or herself

Editorial
an article in a publication expressing the opinion of its editors or publishers

Insight
the capacity to discern the true nature of a situation

Opinion
a belief or conclusion held with confidence, but not substantiated by positive knowledge or proof

Perception
the process, act, or faculty of perceiving; insight, intuition, or knowledge gained by perceiving

Perspective
subjective evaluation of a relative significance; point of view

Résumé
a summary, especially a brief record of one's personal history and experience submitted with a job application

Self-Awareness
an awareness of oneself as an individual entity or personality

Writing About Me, Myself, And I

CONTENT-BASED ACTIVITIES

Social Studies: SELF-AWARENESS

Make an ABC book of your favorite things. Describe your favorite friends, hobbies, people, clothes, songs, etc. Try to include one item for each letter of the alphabet.

Social Studies

Write a speech, an editorial, or a position paper on a social issue about which you feel strongly such as capital punishment, racism, child abuse, teenage suicide, divorce, or curfews for teenagers. Share it in some way by doing one or more of the following:
- writing it in a letter and sending it to someone,
- framing it and placing it in a prominent location,
- wrapping it up as a present and giving it to someone,
- recording it on an audio tape, or
- taping it onto a mirror or preserving it under glass.

Art

Create a number of sketches or drawings showing a series of memorable moments in your life. Arrange these artistically in a collage.

Writing About Me, Myself, And I

CONTENT-BASED ACTIVITIES

Math

Create an Excitement Level Graph of things you are studying in school. On the vertical axis make an excitement range (1-10), and on the horizontal axis number specific themes or topics from your courses. Then plot it. What might your teachers learn from this diagram about their subject matter and their teaching methods?

Science

Design a poster or a brochure supporting an environmental cause for your community about which you personally feel strongly and for which you are willing to work to help make a difference.

Language Arts: WRITING

Choose any three of the following things to write about yourself:
- an announcement of an upcoming event in your life
- an apology to someone you have offended
- a character sketch of someone about whom you care
- a complaint you wish to register
- a contract with someone
- a data sheet of important facts and/or statistics
- an epitaph for your tombstone
- a greeting card for your birthday
- a horoscope for today
- a how-to speech on something you know how to do well
- an opinion on something about which you feel strongly
- a post card to yourself about a place you've been
- a résumé of your skills
- a self-portrait
- a personal tribute
- a "Wanted" poster

Writing About Me, Myself, And I

CONTENT-BASED ACTIVITIES

Optional Extension

You will be compiling your own "Private Book of Lists" that is to serve as a summary of your personal habits, interests, experiences, and wishes. To begin this project, construct a booklet that is approximately 13 inches long and 5 inches wide. Make certain your booklet has a sturdy set of covers and at least 20 pages. Make a title page for your book that includes the title, author's name, publisher, copyright date, and dedication statement.

Now, compile lists in at least ten of the categories outlined below, making certain that your list is a collection of personal preferences.

1. Ten major events in my life
2. Ten people I respect, admire, and will/would listen to
3. Ten issues about which I would argue or debate with my family and friends
4. Ten awards I want to give myself or think I have earned
5. Ten places I want to go or things I want to do in my lifetime
6. Ten things that "bug me" about other people, places, or things
7. Ten jobs I would never want to have
8. Ten careers I would consider for myself
9. Ten ways to get me to smile or laugh
10. Ten foods I would "die for"
11. Ten subjects or topics about which I want to learn more
12. Ten things that frighten me about the future
13. Ten books I would recommend to others
14. Ten possessions I own that are important to me
15. Ten things I would do to redecorate or rearrange my bedroom
16. Ten wishes I have for others less fortunate
17. Ten things I would never want to see or experience
18. Ten things I like about myself
19. Ten things I would buy today if I had the money
20. Ten reasons to stay and do well in school

Writing About Me, Myself, And I

— JOURNALING —

Write about yesterday, from getting up in the morning until bedtime. Be as specific as possible about what occurred during each hour of the day. Then read your journal entry carefully, and underline the high points of the day, circle the things you would do differently if you could relive the day, and star the things you would like to do again today or tomorrow.

_____

_____

_____

_____

_____

_____

_____

_____

_____

_____

_____

_____

_____

_____

_____

_____

_____

_____

_____

_____

_____

_____

_____

_____

_____

_____

Survival Of The Fittest

— UNIT OVERVIEW —

Theme

School Culture And Academic Survival

Purpose

To help students understand the concept of survival as it relates to both the human and the animal world. Visit almost any part of our world, and you'll find people and animal life of some kind living there. These environments are all different and are sometimes harsh or challenging, yet individuals and creatures live in them because their bodies and habits have adapted to their homes.

Content Focus

Science

Assessment

Each student will develop a survival handbook or guide on a topic of his or her own choosing. Each student will also maintain a "Learning Log" that contains daily entries on ideas, questions, findings, activities, and reactions he or she has experienced as part of this interdisciplinary unit.

Specific Objectives

NOTES

1. The student will develop working definitions of "survival" and "adaptation."
2. The student will create a comic strip with a survival theme.
3. The student will research to find ways that animals survive through adaptation in one of the five biomes—Polar Region, Desert, Rain Forest, Savanna, and Mountain Area.
4. The student will complete a survival guide for some aspect of his or her home, school, or community life.
5. The student will compile a bibliography of books with survival themes.
6. The student will engage in a simple simulation that requires decision-making in a survival situation.

Survival Of The Fittest

GLOSSARY

Adaptation
Something that is changed so that it is suitable to a new situation

Biome
A community of living organisms of a single major ecological region

Desert
A dry, barren region

Mountain
A natural elevation of the earth's surface having considerable mass, generally steep sides, and height greater than a hill

Polar Region
The land and water areas surrounding the North and South Poles

Rain Forest
A dense evergreen forest occupying a tropical region with an annual rainfall of at least 100 inches

Savanna
A flat, treeless grassland of tropical, sub-tropical regions

Survival
The act or process of remaining alive

Survival Of The Fittest

CONTENT-BASED ACTIVITIES

Social Studies: SELF-AWARENESS

Look up the words "survival" and "adaptation" in the dictionary and write their definitions in your Learning Log. On a separate piece of manila drawing paper, illustrate these definitions with drawings, sketches, or stick figures showing things you do to adapt and survive during these middle grade years.

Creative Thinking: VISUAL IMAGERY

Create a comic strip featuring a new cartoon character who is surviving one of the following situations:
- a test in science class,
- a first day in a new middle school,
- a ride on the school bus,
- a competition for a team sport,
- a forgotten homework assignment, or
- an overdue report.

Science/Math

Work with a friend to research how the structure of each of these animal bodies can help the animal to obtain food, survive temperature extremes, escape enemies, and/or raise young. Describe your findings in chart or Venn diagram form to show likenesses and differences.

Arctic Fox	Collared Lemming
Musk-ox	Caribou
Penguin	Camel
Roadrunner	Kangaroo Rat
Spider Monkey	Sloth
Giraffe	Grassland Monkey
Baboon	Cheetah
Spanish Ibex	Aardvark
Klipspringer	Chamois
Panda	Pika

Survival Of The Fittest

CONTENT-BASED ACTIVITIES

Study Skills: RESEARCH

Research an animal of your choice from any one of the biomes. Focus on the animal's unique adaptive features for surviving its own special environment. Write a brief report following the simple format shown here. Make a list of facts about the animal to help in the writing of your report.

Animal Name _____

Line 1	Lives	_____
Line 2	Physical trait	_____
Line 3	Physical trait	_____
Line 4	Physical trait	_____
Line 5	Eats	_____
Line 6	Traps (catches) food by	_____
Line 7	Adaptation	_____
Line 8	Adaptation	_____
Line 9	Adaptation	_____
Line 10	Cares for young by	_____
Line 11	Interesting fact	_____
Line 12	Interesting fact	_____

Language Arts: WRITING

Work with a small group of peers to develop a survival handbook or guide on a topic of your choice. Be sure your handbook or guide contains a cover, table of contents, and five to ten pages of good advice or tips for students your age. Some topics for you to consider writing about are:

- A Handbook For Getting Good Grades
- A Handbook For Getting Along With Adults
- A Survival Guide For Staying Out Of Trouble
- A Survival Guide For Students New To Our School
- A Handbook For Keeping Your Body And Mind In Good Shape

Language Arts: READING, WRITING

Browse through the library to locate approximately ten books that have a "survival" theme. Compile a bibliography of these books. Choose one of these books and write in your Learning Log a brief summary of what you think it is about after reviewing the title, chapter headings, and illustrations (if any are included). If time permits, read the book and write a brief review of it in your Learning Log.

Survival
Of The Fittest

── CONTENT-BASED ACTIVITIES ──
┌─ *Optional Extension* ──

Complete the survival "mini-simulation" below according to directions given. After the simulation, complete these starter statements:

1. From this simulation, I learned that . . .
2. The best thing about this activity was . . .
3. Something I found difficult to do in this activity was . . .

SIMULATION GAME

"Be A Space Navigator"

DIRECTIONS: You are the leader of a powerful space vehicle that explores the intergalactic world. How will you plan for your upcoming voyage? Simulate the experience by completing the tasks outlined here.

Task One: List 20 essential items you will need to carry in your spacecraft to keep you and your five crew members alive and healthy.

Task Two: Describe the five crew members you will take with you. What special skills, interests, and experiences do they have? What jobs will they be assigned to perform?

Task Three: Design the interior of the spacecraft to accommodate you and the crew. What does it look like?

Task Four: Design the exterior of the spacecraft to accommodate your ongoing supplies of air, food, and water.

Task Five: Develop a set of rules and regulations for you and your crew to follow that will ensure harmony aboard the spacecraft.

Survival Of The Fittest

— JOURNALING —

Write about a time that you felt your personal survival was threatened. Describe your emotions and tell what you learned from the experience.

_____
_____
_____
_____
_____
_____
_____
_____
_____
_____
_____
_____
_____
_____
_____
_____
_____
_____
_____
_____
_____
_____
_____
_____
_____
_____

Numbers In The News

— UNIT OVERVIEW —

Theme

School Culture And Academic Survival

Purpose

To show students how numbers play an important role in the sharing of information throughout the sections of the newspaper. Students are encouraged to spend ample time browsing through the pages of a newspaper and recording what and how numbers are used to validate everything from facts in news and sports stories to opinions in editorials.

Content Focus

Math

Assessment

The student will plan and write one or more sections of a math classroom newspaper and will maintain a folder of his or her work from the assigned activities.

Specific Objectives

1. The student will examine the following sections of a newspaper to note the use of numbers in the writing and reading of information presented in this media form: index, news section, feature section, sports section, business section, editorial section, comic section, and classified ad section.
2. The student will compile a stock portfolio for one week.
3. The student will use the display ads to plan a personal outing or event.
4. The student will help to plan and produce a classroom newspaper based on the study of math.

NOTES

Numbers In The News

GLOSSARY

Balloon
In a comic strip, the line surrounding a statement to make it look as though the words were coming from a person's mouth

Banner Headline
A large front page headline which sometimes spans the full width of the page

By-Line
A line of copy which identifies by name the writer of an article; usually placed at the beginning of an article

Classified Advertising
Brief advertisements which are divided into categories or classes and run together in the newspaper

Column
A vertical arrangement of copy on a news page

Display Advertising
Advertising that is set off from newspaper text by larger display typefaces, rules, incorporated white spaces, and illustrations

Editorial
Opinionated material which states the viewpoint of a particular newspaper according to its publisher and/or editors

Editorial Cartoon
A cartoon which illustrates a newspaper's editorial stance on an issue

Feature
Newspaper material which deals more with human nature items than with news-oriented items

Front Page
The first sheet or section of a newspaper which is devoted to the most newsworthy stories of the day

Lead
The first paragraph of a news story which summarizes the chief news to follow

Lead Story
The most important front page story, found under the banner headline, that is usually allocated the most extensive coverage

News
Current factual information which is of immediate relevance to readers and viewers of communications media

Straight News
News which is characterized by reported facts and organized according to the inverted pyramid format

Numbers
In The News

CONTENT-BASED ACTIVITIES

Math

Use the index on the front page of the newspaper to locate the different sections that make up your community newspaper. Rewrite each of the page numbers in the index as an equation to be solved by the reader. For example, page 6 might be written as:

$$4 \times (22 - 10) + 6 \div 9 \quad \text{or} \quad \frac{1}{2} \times 12$$

Math

Read through the comics and select five of your favorites. Cut each comic strip apart and mix up the pieces. Give your collection of comic strip sections to a friend who should try to put all of them back in their correct sequences. How is logical reasoning used in this process? Now, write a series of number patterns with at least six to eight frames. Ask a friend to complete the number patterns using the same type of logical reasoning.

Reading/Math

Select a feature article from one of the news stories located in the inside front page section of the newspaper. "Guesstimate" which vowel appears most frequently in the article. Write down your guess and count the vowels to prove or disprove your prediction. Do this with several other articles of similar length. Organize your predictions and results in some type of table.

Critical Thinking

Browse through the front section of the newspaper to locate as many different types of numbers as you can in the news articles presented. Record the numbers and organize them in some meaningful way. Analyze your number results and draw some conclusions about how and why numbers are used to present information in the newspaper. Are there more whole numbers, fractions, decimals, or percentages? Does the type of article influence the type of numbers used in the article?

Numbers In The News

CONTENT-BASED ACTIVITIES

Science/Decision-Making

Work with a small group of friends to study the stock market figures in the business section of the newspaper. Locate and evaluate all of the stocks offered by companies dealing in the earth's natural resources (oil, gas, cattle, grain, etc.). As a group, assemble a mini-portfolio of the stocks that your group would like to buy and own for one week, with an initial investment of $10,000.00 for the group. What stocks will you buy and how many shares of each stock will you purchase? (Consider how each company makes use of the earth's natural resources before making a decision to invest.) At the end of the week, determine the value of your stock dividends. Did they go up or down and by how much?

Social Studies

Review the classified advertising section of the newspaper to note the many different clusters of ads that appear throughout this section. Make a list of these different clusters and cut out one or two ads for each cluster that are of special interest to you because of their messages. Paste these under each cluster label. Next, compose a special classified ad of your own. Determine which cluster it would go under and how much it would cost you to place it in this section. Use the display ads to shop for bargains. Plan a dinner, party, wardrobe, or "day on the town" based on the display ads you find in the newspaper. Create a collage with the ads and the plan for your event!

Language Arts

Record the headlines of articles from the sports section that contain numbers. Underline the verbs in each of these articles. What makes the headlines of articles in this section so different from those in other sections of the newspaper? Create a treasure hunt of numbers from the sports section of the paper for your classmates to complete. Begin this task by selecting eight to ten articles about a sporting event and then writing out a question for each article that involves a number as an answer. For example, if you were reading a sports story about a rowing team, the question might be: "What was the length of the course for the Riverview High School Rowing Club in the recent High School State Rowing Championships held on Lake Mineolo in Clermont, Florida?" (Answer: 1,500 meters)

Numbers
In The News

CONTENT-BASED ACTIVITIES

Language Arts: WRITING

Read through the editorial section of the newspaper including the editorials, letters to the editor, and the editorial cartoons. Notice if and how numbers are used by the editorial writers to reinforce a point or justify an opinion. Compose a short editorial or letter to the editor explaining why numbers can and always should provide documentation for a position the writer is making on an issue.

Optional Extension

Work with the students in your classroom to plan and produce a community newspaper based on math and the activities that take place in your math program. Make certain your newspaper has all of the required sections and focuses on a mathematical theme. Perhaps math contests or games could make up the events in the sports section. Perhaps feature stories about good math students and news stories about daily math lessons could make up the events covered in the front page section. Perhaps a series of cartoon characters featuring math "geniuses" or math "dummies" could make up the comic section. Perhaps creative classified and display ads promoting math tutors or math aids could make up the advertising section. Perhaps math puzzles and brain teasers could serve as fillers for an entertainment section. Don't forget to include a newspaper masthead, index, and editorial section for your math newspaper.

Numbers In The News

JOURNALING

Write a feature article on yourself. (You may use information from your real life for the article, or you may invent a wild adventure about which to write.)

The Community As A School For Learning

Theme

School Culture And Academic Survival

Purpose

To provide students with a variety of ways they can explore and/or contribute to the "health" of their classroom or school community. These activities will actively engage the students in a set of tasks to share what they have learned and to make others part of that learning process.

Content Focus

Math

Assessment

Each student will prepare a scrapbook containing evidence of participation in each of the content-based activities. Pictures, work samples, written descriptions, photographs, or peer reviews may be included in the scrapbook for documentation.

Specific Objectives

NOTES

1. The student will construct a mini-society within the classroom setting in order to simulate the major institutions of a community.
2. The student will participate in a series of learning stations where students become the resident experts in a given subject area.
3. The student will plan a booth for a math carnival and use this as a vehicle for teaching others about a math concept.
4. The student will create plans for a school club that will make some type of contribution to the school community.
5. The student will organize a Parent-Student Exchange Day.

The Community As A School For Learning

GLOSSARY

Bailiff
A court attendant entrusted with such duties as the maintenance of order in a courtroom during a trial

Community
A group of people living in the same locality and under the same government; or a group or class having common interests

Government
The agency or apparatus through which an individual or body that governs exercises its authority and performs its functions

Marketplace
A public place for buying and selling merchandise; the world of business and commerce; or the figurative place of assembly where works, opinions, and ideas are debated and exchanged

Monetary
Of or pertaining to money or its means of circulation

Society
The totality of social relationships among human beings; or a group of human beings broadly distinguished from other groups by mutual interests, participation in characteristic relationships, shared institutions, and a common culture

The Community As A School For Learning

Social Studies

Organize your classroom into a mini-society complete with all the services that any real community would have. Some ideas for you to consider include:

1. Create a Government Council that includes a mayor and a set of council representatives. Elect the mayor and council representatives each marking period or semester. Divide your classroom into groups of four and elect a council member to represent each group. Groups of students should sit together at tables or clusters of desks. Council members meet with the mayor to set classroom laws and fines as well as to plan community events and discuss community concerns.

2. Create a Monetary and Banking System that allows classroom citizens to earn money for completing assignments, holding classroom jobs, helping others, and attending class. Likewise, set up a bank so that each student has his or her own ledger sheet, set of deposit slips, checkbook, and a safe deposit box.

3. Create a Marketplace that encourages student entrepreneurs, lotteries, auctions, and other income producing enterprises such as a post office (postage on all letters between citizens), a rental shop (for borrowing classroom equipment), a tax office (for leasing desk/bulletin board space), or a restaurant (for purchasing snacks).

4. Create a Judicial System that includes a bailiff (who accepts complaints), a jury of five students (to try cases), a core of lawyers (who represent the plaintiff or defendant), and a judge (who makes the sentences).

5. Create a Police System whose members issue tickets and fines for violating classroom rules and who punish repeat offenders by subtracting minutes from their lunch and library time.

Study Skills

Organize a resident-expert system in math (or any other subject area) for students in your class. Divide the material being studied into ten subtopics or skills. Create a set of instruction cards to teach each skill or review each subtopic, a set of practice exercises on transparencies for students to complete, a paper/pencil test to pre- and post-test each student's mastery of the content, and a set of answer keys for self-checking student responses. Set up each skill or subtopic at a learning station and select a student to "captain" the station, making certain that the student understands the material to be learned. Rotate the rest of the students through the stations so that the captain becomes the station's teacher. It is the captain's job to explain the material, provide examples, allow for practice, test for mastery, and reteach concepts not mastered.

The Community As A School For Learning

Math

Divide your math class into small groups and instruct each group to plan a booth for a special math carnival to be held at a later date. The purpose of the math carnival is to design a series of game booths and activities to reinforce basic math concepts that have been learned during the year. To get started, you might want to make a list of possible topics for the game booths. A partial list is given here. Next, you might want to think of a variety of carnival-like games or activity formats with which you are familiar and which also might serve as models for your booth's event. Again, a partial list is given here. In designing your math booth, you might want to:

- design a poster for your booth with the name, rules, and scoring for your math activity,
- purchase, collect, or make lots of little prizes for your booth and devise a point system for awarding them to players,
- agree on a management system for carnival participants to accumulate points from each booth which can be cashed in for bigger prizes at the end of the carnival, and
- serve refreshments that can be purchased with points.

Some possible math topics for booth activities might be: fractions, decimals, estimation, geometry, symmetry, probability, coordinates, word problems, percentages, whole number operations, measurement, money, or logic. Some possible carnival game formats to use might be: bingo, concentration, jeopardy, ring toss, tic-tac-toe, dominoes, hopscotch, checkers, bean bag toss, board games, or relays.

Social Studies/Language Arts

Have you ever thought about forming your own club to make some type of contribution to the school community? All kids like to "belong" to something and a club is a great way to get people together for a common cause or to promote common interests. Work with a group of peers to create a club that will enrich your school community in some meaningful way. Use the outline below to create the plan for your club and see how many members you can attract!

1. What is the primary purpose or goal of your club?
2. What is a possible name, motto, logo, mascot, or handshake for your club?
3. What are the membership requirements for your club and how does one go about joining?
4. What are three possible rules for your club?
5. What kinds of things would you do at your meetings?
6. What are some possible actions you would take, events you would sponsor, or fund-raising tasks you would plan to promote the purpose and goals of your club?

The Community As A School For Learning

Optional Extension

Schedule a special day and invite parents to take their child's place at school for that day. A student may stay home from school only if a parent (or guardian) fills his or her seat in each class. Parents who are separated or divorced may split the day. If parent and child agree to make the exchange, the parent is responsible for all schoolwork the child is expected to do that day whether it is to give a report in social studies or take a test in English. Students issue invitations to the Exchange Day at least one month in advance and prepare an Information Packet that contains the student's schedule, homeroom number, locker combination, homework assignments, dress code, classroom rules, etc.

Note: This idea was suggested by Principal Joe Pius at St. Clair Middle School in St. Clair, Michigan.

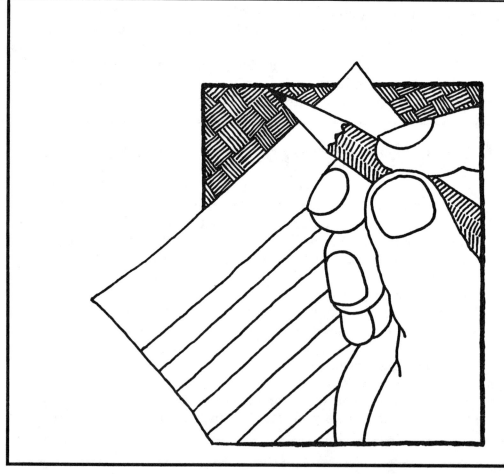

44

The Community As A School For Learning

Think about the leadership role you would most like to assume in a class-room mini-society. Would you want to be mayor, council member, law enforcement officer, banker, judge, merchant, tax assessor, etc.? Write a letter of application for your chosen position, stating the traits and talents you possess that would qualify you for the position and telling how you would fulfill its responsibilities.

_____

_____

_____

_____

_____

_____

_____

_____

_____

_____

_____

_____

_____

_____

_____

_____

_____

_____

_____

_____

_____

_____

_____

_____

_____

Color
My World

UNIT OVERVIEW

Theme

Self-Concept And Relationships

Purpose

To use color as a springboard for viewing the world through the lens of a rainbow. Because color represents a familiar concept and serves as an appealing theme for all students, it can become an effective tool for integration of subject matter and for meeting the students' cognitive and affective needs.

Content Focus

Science

Assessment

Each student will develop a "color" portfolio that contains a variety of artifacts representative of his or her work in this area.

Specific Objectives

NOTES

1. The student will read a book related to the world of color.
2. The student will construct a color self-portrait.
3. The student will design an anti-coloring book page for a class book.
4. The student will create a color poem.
5. The student will engage in a series of color-related math, science, social studies, and language arts activities.

Color
My World

GLOSSARY

Hue
A range of color tints distinct from others; shade

Lens
A carefully ground or molded piece of glass, plastic, or other transparent material with opposite surfaces which are curved, by means of which light rays are refracted so that they converge or diverge to form an image

Prism
A crystalline, transparent solid, with triangular bases and rectangular sides, used to produce or analyze a continuous spectrum

Rainbow
An arc of spectral color appearing in the sky opposite the sun as a result of the refractive dispersion of sunlight in drops of rain or mist

Visual
Serving, resulting from, or pertaining to the sense of sight

Color My World

CONTENT-BASED ACTIVITIES

Language Arts: READING/ART

Read the book entitled *Harold and the Purple Crayon* by Crockett Johnson. After completing the story, draw a picture of your favorite person, place, thing, adventure, experience, vacation spot, activity, or event that you would be willing to share with the class and display on the bulletin board. You are to use your favorite crayon in this drawing and title your picture _____ *and the* _____ *Crayon.*

                                (your name)   *(your color)*

Social Studies: SELF-AWARENESS

We are often asked to keep diaries, write autobiographies, or relate personal experiences in the classroom, but rarely are we asked to paint or draw a self-portrait. Try to think artistically about "who you are" and "what you are like" by responding to these "visually-oriented" questions.

1. If you were to paint a self-portrait, what style of painting would it be? Consider famous artists and their respective periods in art history.
2. What hues and colors would be dominant? Consider pastels, bold shades, blurred color lines, or blacks and grays.
3. What type of setting would you portray? Consider the country, city, beach, mountains, forest, desert, or a rural environment.
4. Who would be the central figures and what would they be doing? Consider an action scene or a pastoral pose.
5. What special symbols, objects, or signs would you want to appear in the foreground or the background? Consider anything from your zodiac sign to a family crest.
6. What unique mat and frame combination would you have to hold your portrait? Consider a wood, plastic, ceramic, metal, rattan, fabric, or gilded frame.

Can you draw this self-portrait or commission someone else to do it for you?

Creative Thinking/Art

Think about the coloring books you had as a young child. The pictures were drawn for you and it was your job to color in the lines. Today's coloring books provide the child with only a partial drawing and a challenging question or direction for the child to follow in completing the drawing. You are to design an original page for a Classroom Anti-Coloring Book that can be distributed to younger students in the school or community. What will your page look like?

Color My World

CONTENT-BASED ACTIVITIES

Language Arts: CREATIVE WRITING

Write an original cinquain based on your favorite color by following the pattern below:
Line 1: Name of your color in big letters
Line 2: Two descriptive adjectives that describe the color
Line 3: Three unusual nouns that name things which are that color
Line 4: Two action verbs which to you are reflective of that color
Line 5: Synonym or another hue for that color

Social Studies: HISTORY

Color names have often been used to describe significant people, places, and things throughout history. Research to find out the answers to each of these color-coded questions:
1. Who were the "Red Coats" and in which war did they fight?
2. Who is known as the "father of the blues"?
3. What is "yellow journalism"?
4. Who were the king and queen of England who began their reign as the "House of Orange"?
5. To what does the "village green" refer?

Math

Cut out sixteen squares of identical size from a piece of manila drawing paper. Color four squares red; color four squares blue; color four squares yellow; and color four squares green. Rearrange these sixteen squares in one big square with four squares across and four squares down so that no similar color appears in the same row, the same column, or on the same diagonal.

Science

Experiment to find out how many different colors you can create by mixing together two or more of these four colors: blue, red, yellow, and black. Record your results in chart or graph form.

Color
My World

── CONTENT-BASED ACTIVITIES ──

── *Optional Extension* ──

Complete one or more of these color activities:

BLUE: Design a blue flag for a blue island that is surrounded by blue water. Write a tourist slogan for the island in blue letters.

PURPLE: Invent a new American holiday that celebrates the color purple on an annual basis. Describe its origin, traditions, rituals, and symbols.

YELLOW: Create a business name, location, logo, and slogan for a corporation that sells only yellow products.

RED: Write a story telling about a time when you woke up one morning and found everything in the world was colored red. What problems did this cause?

GREEN: Compile a geographical dictionary that lists at least 20 different places (cities, countries, bodies of water, mountains, landmarks, etc.) with the word "green" in them. Write a brief entry for each place describing something about its location and/or importance.

ORANGE: Invent and describe in detail a new and versatile orange product that will "take the world by storm."

BROWN: Design and construct a brown paper bag puppet and use it to teach others about conservation of trees.

Color My World

— JOURNALING —

"It's a blue day."
"Everything looks black."
"The whole world is rose-colored."
"I saw red."

Select one of these statements to use as a springboard to write about a feeling you have had recently and the event (or events) which caused your feeling.

_____

_____

_____

_____

_____

_____

_____

_____

_____

_____

_____

_____

_____

_____

_____

_____

_____

_____

_____

_____

_____

The Talents, Traditions, And Trademarks Of Americana Over Time

— UNIT OVERVIEW —

Theme

Self-Concept And Relationships

Purpose

To examine selected aspects of the American culture over time in order to uncover some of the talents, traditions, and trademarks of its continued growth and success. Students will reflect on such elements as America's language, literature, music, crafts, heroes, and art in order to better understand their own American heritage.

Content Focus

Social Studies

Assessment

The student will complete one of the following Americana projects and design a rubric to be used in its evaluation by the teacher and a small group of peers: ABC Book, Americana Poster, or a One Week Vacation Trip in the United States.

Specific Objectives

1. The student will investigate the early crafts of Colonial America.

2. The student will discover how slang words evolve from historical events.

3. The student will research a famous American hero of his or her choice and present the information as part of a monologue.

4. The student will collect quotes from history and interpret their meaning.

5. The student will plan a one-week trip to an American city.

6. The student will make an ABC book about famous American scientists and their contributions.

7. The student will plan and participate in an All-American Day for the class.

The Talents, Traditions, And Trademarks Of Americana Over Time

GLOSSARY

Fad
A fashion that is taken up with great enthusiasm for a brief period of time

Folk Tale
A traditional, usually anonymous, story handed down orally among a people

Monologue
A long speech made by one person, often monopolizing conversation

Patriotism
Love of and devotion to one's country

Primer
An elementary textbook

Slang
The informal vocabulary of a given culture, consisting typically of arbitrary and often temporary coinages and figures of speech

Traditions
Elements of a culture passed down from generation to generation

The Talents, Traditions, And Trademarks Of Americana Over Time

CONTENT-BASED ACTIVITIES

Study Skills: RESEARCH

If you could have been one of the following types of colonial craftsmen, which one would you have chosen to be? Blacksmith, Miller, Weaver, Barber, Hatter, Innkeeper, Cooper, Sawyer, Tanner, Locksmith, Tinsmith, Candlemaker, Baker, Apothecary, Cutler, Shoemaker, or General Store Owner.

1. Choose one of these that sounds interesting and find out more about the trade—type of building needed, tools required, education or skills desired, nature/design of finished product, problems encountered. Take notes on your research.
2. Design a trade sign to hang outside the shop about which you have chosen to study.
3. Make a catalog to show your wares and describe your shop or place of business to others. Show a sketch of your place of business, pictures of your wares, and brief descriptions of each major item (including the cost).

Language Arts: VOCABULARY

Many words or expressions come to us through history. Some examples of these are: Bloomers, Bobby Soxer, Carpetbaggers, Copperhead, Fence Sitting, Gerrymander, Ku Kluxism, Logrolling, Lynch, Maverick, Yankee, Yellow Journalism. See if you can find out how each of these words came into existence, how it was used, and what the same word used today might imply.

Now, work with a partner to make a list of as many slang words as you can which are popular with kids today. Next, make a HIPTIONARY by putting each word into dictionary form, showing its meaning, its pronunciation, its syllabic breakdown, its definition, antonyms or synonyms for it, and its use in a complete sentence.

Creative Thinking: DRAMA

Choose a famous American from history, then do some research to find out what type of person that individual was and what important things he or she did for the country. Once you have gathered enough information, try writing a monologue or one-way conversation about a subject of importance to your character. For example, you might write a dialogue as Betsy Ross telling a group of women how she designed the American flag; or you might be Ben Franklin talking to a group of men about his kite-flying experiences with electricity. Once you have finished your research and your monologue, deliver the speeches as if YOU were indeed that character from history.

The Talents, Traditions, And Trademarks Of Americana Over Time

CONTENT-BASED ACTIVITIES

Social Studies: HISTORY

Collect as many famous historical quotations from your reading as you can (social studies books, library resource books, books of famous sayings, etc.). As you find a quote that has meaning for you, write it down, and answer the following questions about it: Who said it? When and where was it said? Why was it said? What were the circumstances? In your own words, can you tell what it means? Can you explain what this quote has that is appealing?

Now . . . work these quotations you've collected into a poem, a monologue, a skit, or a short story. Be as original and as clever as you can.

Geography/Math

Use a United States map to find examples of each of the following geographical features: mountain range, national park, desert, peninsula, bay, cliff, canyon, gulf, island, lake, ocean, river, strait, and valley. Now . . . choose a city to visit during a one-week vacation. Organize the trip by days so that you include the following information for each day:

DAY ONE: • Total number of miles traveled
              • Historical sights visited
              • Major routes taken (highways, cities)
              • Place where you spent the night

After your trip is completely planned, figure out the following:
              • Total number of miles traveled
              • Total car expenses (figure 20¢/mile)
              • Total food expenses (figure $20.00/day/person)
              • Total motel expenses (figure $35.00/day/person)
              • Miscellaneous expenses for trip (fees, souvenirs)
              • TOTAL COST OF TRIP

Science

Make an ABC booklet about famous American scientists. Each page should contain an idea that an American scientist has contributed to American culture that begins with a letter of the alphabet. The idea should then be explained so that the reader learns something about the idea being presented.

The Talents, Traditions, And Trademarks Of Americana Over Time

CONTENT-BASED ACTIVITIES

Optional Extension

Get a group of your classmates together and plan an All-American Day. Perhaps each member of your group or your class will want to be responsible for planning a particular activity. Some suggestions for you to consider are:

1. Assign every student the name of a famous American for the day.
2. Lunch—Prepare an all-American menu or some old-fashioned snacks.
3. Reading— Try designing a lesson that is based on American folk tales, tall tales, or biographies.
4. Spelling—Try an old-fashioned spelling bee or spell down.
5. Social Studies—Design some type of game that involves map skills, research, or collages based on some aspect of American geography.
6. Science—Create a set of simple experiments that demonstrate some basic scientific principles developed by American inventors.
7. Music—Hold an old-fashioned sing-along, or play records of music representative of different periods of American history.
8. Art—Make modern-day versions of hornbooks, primers, quill pens, sampler bookmarks, or old-fashioned toys.
9. Physical Education—Learn how to play some Colonial games or hold a square dance.

The Talents, Traditions, And Trademarks Of Americana Over Time

JOURNALING

Divide a sheet of paper into several sections of varying shapes and sizes. In each of these sections, put ideas, facts, creative writing, research data, and anything else you've collected about America so that the finished poster reflects YOU and YOUR FEELINGS towards your country. Some possible topics to include as part of your poster might be:

- Favorite American quotations
- Song lyrics about America
- ABC facts about America, acrostic style
- Three wishes for your country
- Predictions for America's future
- Evidence of what it means to be an American

Write your notes for the poster here.

_____

_____

_____

_____

_____

_____

_____

_____

_____

_____

_____

_____

_____

_____

_____

_____

_____

_____

_____

_____

What Insects Can Teach Us About Life

UNIT OVERVIEW

Theme

Self-Concept And Relationships

Purpose

To use the insect as a model for looking at community concepts as part of both the human and non-human world. Creatures such as bees and ants have always functioned as a community in preserving their "culture" and are interesting subjects to study with this idea in mind. This unit also attempts to examine other members of the insect world that are less popular in the perceptions of many—insects such as roaches and fleas—and are, therefore, counterproductive to the community notion.

Content Focus

Science

Assessment

The student will develop a series of products that demonstrate creative ways of looking at the insect world according to guidelines given for this purpose.

Specific Objectives

1. The student will examine the characteristics, functions, and structures of selected members of the insect world that demonstrate a sense of community in their lifestyle.

2. The student will examine the characteristics, functions, and structures of selected members of the insect world who do not demonstrate a sense of community in their lifestyle.

3. The student will read both fiction and nonfiction selections in literature that use insects as the significant characters or references in the story or as information sources.

4. The student will engage in research to find out more about the behavior of insects.

5. The student will create an imaginary insect that has its own unique characteristics, habits, structures, and lifestyle.

What Insects Can Teach Us About Life

GLOSSARY

Abdomen
In arthropods, the major posterior part of the body

Antenna
One of the paired, flexible, jointed sensory appendages on the head of an insect

Colony
A group of the same kind of animals living or growing together

Life Cycle
The course of developmental changes through which an organism passes from its inception to the mature state, especially a progression through a series of differing stages of development, as in insect metamorphosis

Lifestyle
A way of living or maintaining life shared by a community

Thorax
The second or middle region of the body of an arthropod, in insects bearing the true legs and wings

What Insects Can Teach Us About Life

CONTENT-BASED ACTIVITIES

Science/Creative Thinking/Art

Ants live in large groups called colonies. Colony members have many different jobs to perform. The queen lays eggs; the workers excavate tunnels, gather food, and take care of the nest; the soldiers defend the colony. Ants come in a variety of colors: black, brown, reddish, or brownish-yellow.

1. Invent a caricature of the queen ant. Be imaginative and include a simple biography of her life to date.
2. Imagine you are a soldier ant reporting for duty. Describe your uniform, weaponry, and training exercises for attack.

Science/Creative Thinking/Writing

Fleas are found on many different animals, including cats and dogs. They can also live in carpeting and vacuum cleaners. Fleas' bodies are flat and narrow, and they are able to move quickly through an animal's hair. Fleas are among the greatest jumpers in the insect world. Their long hind legs have enlarged coxae which help them leap a distance of a foot or more.

1. Pretend you are a flea who has lived a lifetime in the fur of a famous dog or cat. Write your autobiography entitled:"The Life and Times of _____ ." Give information about your birth, home, family history, hobbies, occupations, travels, education, friends, special talents, and the special circumstances of your death.
2. Invent a "mini-vacuum cleaner" for removing fleas from animals. Create an advertisement telling the world about it.

Science/Creative Thinking/Math

Centipedes are found inside houses, running along floors, baseboards, and walls at remarkable speeds. Centipedes also like dark places outside and can be found under stones, under houses, in cracks, and in leaf mold. Centipedes are born with only seven pairs of legs, but the number increases to 15 as it grows.

1. Pretend you own a shoe store that caters to centipedes. Show several shoe designs that are popular with today's centipede.
2. Describe a conversation between two athletes who are competing with one another in the Insect Olympics. What might a centipede say about his speed to a flea about her jumping ability and vice versa?
3. Make up three math story problems about centipedes and their many legs. Ask a friend to solve your problems.

What Insects Can Teach Us About Life

CONTENT-BASED ACTIVITIES
Science/Creative Thinking/Health

Cockroaches eat almost anything people eat, most often coming out at night to look for their food. Most cockroaches move about freely, even on smooth surfaces such as appliances and tile floors, because they have sticky pads on their legs. It is difficult to kill all cockroaches in a house because the female lays her eggs in well-hidden places. Cockroaches can spread disease and are among the world's oldest insects.

1. Imagine you are the talk show host of a new show about insects for insects. Interview the world's oldest roach.
2. Research to find out as much information as you can about the cockroach and make up a series of questions about how they influence the health of human beings in your community.

Language Arts: READING

1. Aesop's fables include several fables about insects. Locate one of these fables and act out the story with your friends.
2. Browse through the media center to compile a list of fiction books that have "bugs" in them. Be sure to include novels (*Charlotte's Web*) as well as picture books of both realism and fantasy.
3. Read the book *Demi's Secret Garden*, a beautiful book of poems compiled and illustrated by Demi (published by Henry Holt and Company). Write a review of this book, highlighting its unusual characteristics.

Social Studies

It has been said that insects are creatures who exhibit an extreme sense of community when it comes to supporting one another's chance for survival. Colonies of both bees and ants are prime examples of how the community concept functions successfully in terms of work roles and life roles that are designed to promote a reasonable life cycle for its inhabitants.

1. Research to find out all that you can about the structure and/or organization of the bee and the ant colonies. Use this information to create a "speech" from an insect's perspective to persuade the human species to adapt some of the ways of the insect world in building a better sense of community for the future. You might also want to include in your speech some examples of less popular "insect characteristics" which actually detract from the community idea, using what you know about roaches and fleas.
2. Draw a diagram of the underground world of an ant colony modernizing it for the 21st century by incorporating some human and technological characteristics in its design.

What Insects Can Teach Us About Life

CONTENT-BASED ACTIVITIES

Optional Extension

An insect has a body made of three parts called a thorax, a head, and an abdomen. The thorax contains one or two pairs of wings and three pairs of legs. The head of an insect always has eyes, antennae, and mouthparts designed for biting, sucking, piercing, sipping, or lapping.

1. Create a new insect never before detected. Draw a picture of what it looks like and describe its lifestyle, including food source, habitat, and victims.

2. Plan a bug reunion for all of the insects described in this learning center including your own original "Insectabet." Tell a story about the meeting of these insect characters and record conversations describing what they say to each other. Who is most likely to become friends and who is most likely to be the fierce enemy of the others?

3. Research to find out information about another insect of your own choosing. Write a "critter riddle" about the insect following this pattern:

   a. Write one line that describes its setting.
   b. Write one line that describes its appearance or form.
   c. Start a new line and write about its eyes and feet.
   d. Write two lines that tell what it feels while waiting for something to happen.
   e. Write another two lines that include a sound in the background that upsets your critter and that describes how your critter reacts. See if others can guess what insect you are describing.

What Insects Can Teach Us About Life

— JOURNALING —

Based on your thoughts about insects as a part of a living community, write about the various communities of which you are a part (home, school, city or town, etc.). Identify and explain your role in each community. (What part do you play? What is your contribution to the overall group? What influence does each community have on your personal life?)

_____

_____

_____

_____

_____

_____

_____

_____

_____

_____

_____

_____

_____

_____

_____

_____

_____

_____

_____

_____

_____

_____

_____

_____

_____

Math Is A Ball When Done At the Mall

— UNIT OVERVIEW —

Theme

Problem-Solving And Decision-Making

Purpose

To use the attraction of the typical shopping center or mall as the major spring-board for application of a variety of math and consumer skills. Marketing statistics show that teenagers today spend a great deal of time at the local mall visiting the video arcades, socializing in the fast food courts, patronizing the movie theaters, and shopping at the discount stores. It makes sense, then, to use this popular "hangout" as a source for investigating mathematical concepts in the real world while practicing those same math skills in a realistic context.

Content Focus

Math

Assessment

The student will maintain a learning log of activities, observations, conclusions, and completed assignments at the mall.

Specific Objectives

1. The student will observe shoppers entering and exiting a mall and draw some conclusions about their preferred traffic patterns.
2. The student will examine a floor plan of a mall to determine which types of stores have the highest percentages of floor space.
3. The student will analyze the stores in a mall to develop ratios of stores that sell products to stores that provide a service.
4. The student will discover the methods used by retailers to attract customers in their stores.
5. The student will design an ideal mall for kids based on their unique needs and characteristics.
6. The student will plan a food budget for a day and do a comparison shopping of the best food values available in a mall.
7. The student will develop a plan for attracting new customers to the mall.
8. The student will develop a series of special features or events to be held at a mall over the course of one year.
9. The student will organize a "Value Treasure Hunt" at a mall.

Math Is A Ball When Done At the Mall

GLOSSARY

Advertising
the action of attracting public attention to a product or business

Customer
a person who buys goods or services

Marketing
the commercial functions involved in transferring goods from producer to consumer

Personnel
the body of persons employed by or active in an organization, business, or service

Producer
a person or organization that grows or manufactures goods or services for sale

Product
something produced by human or mechanical effort or by a natural process

Retail
the sale of goods or commodities in small quantities to the consumer

Service
work done for others as an occupation or business

Statistician
a mathematician specializing in statistics

Math Is A Ball When Done At the Mall

CONTENT-BASED ACTIVITIES

Creative Thinking/Problem-Solving

Work with a group of students to "check out" all of the mall entrances and exits. Together, develop a plan for determining which of these is the busiest and most convenient for mall customers. Make certain that your plan provides for:
- division of labor so that every mall entrance/exit has a student observer,
- method for tallying customers as they enter and exit the mall during a given time period (preferably during the mall's busiest hours),
- procedures for graphing results of tallies and observations, and
- procedures for drawing conclusions about why some entrances and exits of the mall are more popular with patrons than others.

Math

Work with a partner to examine the basic floor plan of the mall. Use the mall directory to help you determine all of the different types of stores that occupy the mall's retail space. Determine the percentages of floor space given to each type or category of retail outlet. Show these results in chart form. Use this information to classify each of the mall's retail spaces as a "Producer of Goods" or a "Producer of Services." Determine the ratio of producers of services with producers of goods. Can you break these figures down further to generate additional ratios of store types or categories?

Social Studies

Walk through the mall and record all of the different ways that store owners and mall personnel market their products and services. What strategies do they use to attract people to the mall, in the stores, and to purchase goods or services? Consider media advertising, sale flyers and signs, mall exhibits and shows, window displays, product showcases, strolling sales clerks, etc. Prepare a marketing report that summarizes your findings.

Language Arts: WRITING

Pretend that you are a famous developer of shopping centers for kids. You have been commissioned to design a mall in your community that serves kids from birth through age 18. What unusual name, floor plan, physical structures, retail outlets, products, services, attractions, and marketing techniques will you include? Create a booklet outlining all of your ideas, sketches, plans, and proposals for this exciting new mall.

Math Is A Ball When Done At the Mall

CONTENT-BASED ACTIVITIES

Science

A popular part of every mall is its food court, or collection of restaurants. Conduct a survey to determine the diversity of food outlets and the variety of food offerings. What type of cuisine is served most frequently and how do food costs compare from restaurant to restaurant. Work with a friend to establish a food budget for a "day at the mall." Plan your menu for breakfast, lunch, and dinner and then shop around to get the "most for your money." Be sure to include healthy food choices as part of the criteria used for judging good value. What types of restaurants offer the healthiest choices? What foods give you the best value for the money? What features are you paying for other than food, if any?

Creative Thinking

Today's shopping malls are becoming more than a collection of stores in which to shop. Many of them have video arcades, movie theaters, and day care centers that service mall customers and that provide income for vendors. Work with a group of friends to think of some unusual and unique features that a mall could have to attract new consumers and better meet the needs of regular customers. Some ideas to consider might be a shopping mall that has a public library, a roller skating rink, or a stage for live performances. Develop a plan for including one or more of your new features in a mall by determining what space needs it would require, what optional services it would offer, and what prices it would charge.

Creative Thinking/Writing

Shopping centers often try to attract customers by staging special events during their busy hours such as art and craft shows, health fairs, and antique bazaars. Pretend you are the manager of a large mall in your community and it is your job to feature a series of events for a full year. Develop a "Calendar of Special Attractions" that advertises an unusual activity for each month. Briefly describe each one in an attractive flyer that could be sent out in a mailing at the beginning of the year.

Math Is A Ball When Done At the Mall

CONTENT-BASED ACTIVITIES

Optional Extension

Shopping centers compete with one another by trying to offer better values to their customers. Work with a group of friends to conduct a "Value Treasure Hunt" at your favorite mall posing as a "hidden shopper" and searching for the best values you can find. To begin this activity, decide on your group's definition of "best value." Once you have agreed upon the criteria for "value," conduct a search to determine the following "best value" items:

- Best Value in Food
- Best Value in Entertainment
- Best Value in Service
- Best Value in Merchandise

Outline the script for a television feature article highlighting the mall's special attractions.

Math Is A Ball When Done At the Mall

JOURNALING

Write about a perfect day at the mall of your dreams. Who would be with you? What shops and services would be available and how would you use them? What would you buy? How much money would you need?

_____

_____

_____

_____

_____

_____

_____

_____

_____

_____

_____

_____

_____

_____

_____

_____

_____

_____

_____

_____

_____

_____

_____

_____

Voting: The Rewards And Responsibilities Of Citizenship

— UNIT OVERVIEW —

Theme

Problem-Solving And Decision-Making

Purpose

To examine the role of the office of the presidency and the act of voting as essential elements for promoting citizenship among young people throughout the United States. Because young people can vote at age 18, it is important that the students in middle school begin developing an understanding of the electoral college and an appreciation for the election process.

Content Focus

Social Studies

Assessment

The student will maintain a portfolio of work that represents the assignments completed as part of this interdisciplinary unit. The student will also take an active part in a mock classroom election and be able to share his or her reflections about this event in a small group discussion.

Specific Objectives

1. The student will research the background of past presidents of the United States and draw some conclusions about common elements in their backgrounds.
2. The student will construct a time line of landmark voting decisions.
3. The student will examine the office of the presidency and the steps for electing a president.
4. The student will be able to describe the Electoral College.
5. The student will identify national symbols and philosophies of the two major political parties in the United States.
6. The student will identify today's social, economic, and political issues, individuals, and organizations that have an impact on today's political process.
7. The student will develop a plan for getting elected to a mock office and will participate in a mock classroom election.

Voting: The Rewards And Responsibilities Of Citizenship

── GLOSSARY ──

Campaign
The operation undertaken to attain political office before an election

Congressman
A member of the U. S. House of Congress, especially the House of Representatives

Democrats
Members of the Democratic Party, one of the two major political parties in the United States, originating in 1828

Electoral College
A body of electors chosen to elect the president and vice president of the United States

Inauguration
A formal introduction to office

Itinerary
the route or proposed route of a journey

Politics
the activities or affairs of a government, politician, or political party

Polls
The place where votes are cast and registered

Republicans
Members of the Republican Party, the other of the two major political parties in the United States, organized in 1854

U. S. Representative
A member of the U.S. House of Representatives, the lower house of the U.S. Congress, to which members are elected from each state in numbers proportional to state population

U. S. Senator
A member of the upper house of the U.S. Congress, to which two members are elected from each state

Voting: The Rewards And Responsibilities Of Citizenship

CONTENT-BASED ACTIVITIES

Study Skills: RESEARCH

Research the background of any ten past presidents in terms of their education, religion, age when elected, ethnic heritage, military service, careers/occupations, marital status, and political party membership. Write the results of your research in chart form. What conclusions can you draw about the type of person who is most likely to be elected president?

Social Studies

Make a time line of important dates and brief explanations of events and people related to the history of voting. Add illustrations to your work.

Social Studies

Make a series of matching flash cards—some with special election, political, or government terms on them, and the others with corresponding definitions. Use these to play a game of Concentration.

Language Arts: CREATIVE EXPRESSION

Research to find out all you can about the office of the presidency. Use this information as the basis for developing an informative booklet with a cartoon format that could be used to instruct people in your community.

Critical Thinking

Find out all you can about the Electoral College. What is it? What does it do? How many electors are there? What determines the number? Write your findings in paragraph form. Then decide what key states you would want to concentrate on in a campaign for president. Outline a good strategy for setting up an effective campaign in these states.

Voting: The Rewards And Responsibilities Of Citizenship

CONTENT-BASED ACTIVITIES

Study Skills: OUTLINING

Design a creative flow chart or diagram to outline the various steps to the presidency. Be sure to include such things as primary election, national convention, nomination, campaign, vote, meeting of electors, inaugural ceremonies, etc. Create a colorful, informative, simple, and symbolic flow chart or diagram.

Art

If this were an election year, what would the key campaign issues most likely be? Use a series of newspaper articles to support your choices. Display your work in some way: poster, mural, collage, scroll, or booklet form.

Social Studies: GEOGRAPHY

Get a map of the United States and plot an ideal presidential campaign trip if you were indeed trying to hit only the key states in terms of the Electoral College. Draw lines on the map from one spot to the next. What cities or states would you visit? How much time would you spend in each place? What kinds of things would you do or talk about in each area? Write a complete itinerary for your campaign.

Science

How much responsibility should the president of the United States have for conservation of the nation's natural resources? Interview at least ten people of all ages to answer this question. Use the results to write an essay on the topic.

Social Studies

Set up a panel discussion to explore one of the following topics:
- The Job Of President Is Too Big For One Person
- Politicians Are Not All Bad
- It Is Time For A Female President
- The 18-Year-Old Vote Is A Good Thing
- Limiting The President To One Six-Year Term
- Impeachment As A Common Practice

Voting: The Rewards And Responsibilities Of Citizenship

CONTENT-BASED ACTIVITIES

Math

Prepare a simple quiz of true/false, fill-in-the-blanks, or multiple choice questions on the topic of elections, politics, or the presidency. Give it to a group of people including students, teachers, parents, and citizens of the community. How informed are people in general? Which group is most informed? Least informed? Tally your results and record them on a graph.

Creative Thinking

The U. S. has two major political parties—Democrats and Republicans. Each party has some basic differences. Research to find out what these differences are in terms of:
- type of person party tends to attract • national symbols used • today's key leaders
- current number in House and Senate • basic philosophy

Now . . . invent a third party of your own explaining how your party differs from the two current parties.

Language Arts: WRITING

Write a personal letter to one of your state Senators or Representatives asking him or her some questions about a concern you have as a junior citizen. Be specific in both your comments and questions.

Creative Thinking/Writing

Suppose you were running for an office in some club, organization, or group in your school. Design a complete campaign for getting yourself elected including a handbill, school newspaper ad, announcement to be read over the public address system, campaign button or patch, slogan, and some type of personal speech. Write your inaugural speech to tell the world what you will do when elected.

Social Studies

Help your teacher set up a mock classroom election for class officers. Try to include all aspects of a presidential election in your plans including a primary, a national convention, a campaign, a vote, and a swearing-in ceremony.

Voting: The Rewards And Responsibilities Of Citizenship

JOURNALING

Pretend you are a political candidate today for an important office. Outline a plan aimed at getting the 18-year-old vote. What would you do? Where would you go? What promises would you make? How would you get them to the polls? What image would you personally want to project? What things would you avoid? Write a journal entry addressing these issues and concerns.

_____

_____

_____

_____

_____

_____

_____

_____

_____

_____

_____

_____

_____

_____

_____

_____

_____

_____

_____

_____

_____

_____

_____

_____

_____

Ways To Make Every Day Earth Day

— UNIT OVERVIEW —

Theme

Problem-Solving And Decision-Making

Purpose

To make students more aware of their environment and the concerns that are associated with it. Students will research a wide range of environmental problems, compile information about environmental issues, and learn about a number of environmental concepts.

Content Focus

Science

Assessment

The student will create an exhibit or display of his or her work generated through the activities of this interdisciplinary unit.

Specific Objectives

1. The student will plan a tour of environmental problem areas in his or her school or community.
2. The student will develop, administer, and compile results of a conservation quiz and survey to determine the E.Q. (Environmental Quotient) of selected students and adults.
3. The student will view a common environmental problem through the eyes of a person or personified place or thing.
4. The student will plan a classroom or school Puzzle Fair based on an environmental theme.
5. The student will compile an annotated bibliography of picture books that teach others about the environment.
6. The student will identify "seven wonders of the world" that involve some aspect of the environment.
7. The student will write an essay on some aspect of his or her environmental perspective.
8. The student will design a weekly, monthly, or yearly calendar about the environment.
9. The student will create and solve a variety of mathematical word problems that deal with the environment or creatures of the environment.
10. The student will complete a collaborative research project that investigates ten different environmental issues.

Ways To Make
Every Day Earth Day

GLOSSARY

Acid Rain
Acid precipitation falling as rain, abnormally high in sulfuric and nitric acid content that is caused by industrial pollution

Ecology
The relationship between organisms and their environment

Global Warming
The effect created by the earth's atmosphere in trapping heat from the sun, whereby the atmosphere acts like a greenhouse

Landfill
Land in which garbage and trash has been buried

Litter
A disorderly accumulation of carelessly discarded waste materials or scraps

Pollution
The contamination of soil, water, or the atmosphere by the discharge of harmful substances

Recycling
To use garbage or waste again by reprocessing, reconditioning, or adapting to a new use or function

Ways To Make Every Day Earth Day

CONTENT-BASED ACTIVITIES

Social Studies

Design a detailed tour of the environment of your school or local community. Determine what environmental sites and problems exist that need to be addressed through some type of political or social action. Draw a map of the environmental area to be observed and outline a walking or driving tour of it on the map. Include a legend for the map and a brief description of each environmental location with its corresponding issue or problem to be solved.

Math

Create both a conservation quiz and an environmental survey to determine the E. Q. (Environmental Quotient) of people who live and work in your school community. To do this, first construct a set of objective questions to ask others about the conservation of natural resources. Your questions should all be of one type—either true/false, multiple choice, or short answer—but should reflect many different environmental topics. Next, construct a survey of questions to ask others about their habits and methods for protecting the environment. How do they cut down on waste, litter, or pollution? Administer both the quiz and the survey to at least twenty people. Compile the results and show them in graph form. Is there a correlation between how much people know about the environment and how much they work to protect the environment?

Language Arts/Creative Thinking

It is often helpful to view an environmental problem from a perspective other than your own. The use of "personification" can help one do this in a creative and enlightening way. Write a short story from the viewpoint of a victim who has been threatened by environmental abuse. Choose your topic from those suggested here:

1. How would you feel if you were a fish in a polluted mountain stream?
2. How would you feel if you were a river who had a factory dumping toxic waste in your waters on a regular basis?
3. How would you feel if you were a beach whose sands were damaged from an oil spill?
4. How would you feel if you were a tree in a rain forest whose habitat was being burned to make room for a cattle ranch?
5. How would you feel if you were a bird in a meadow whose song could no longer be heard over the noise of construction equipment clearing the land for a business park?
6. How would you feel if you were a ray of sunshine who could never reach the ground because of polluted air from a garbage dump?

Ways To Make Every Day Earth Day

CONTENT-BASED ACTIVITIES

Math

Create and collect a wide range of puzzles related to the environment. These puzzles can include jigsaw puzzles, word finder puzzles, crossword puzzles, maze puzzles, tangram puzzles, number puzzles, word puzzles, game puzzles, dot-to-dot puzzles, and imagination puzzles. Host a Puzzle Mania Party and set up puzzle stations all over the classroom. Establish time limits for solving the puzzles at each station. Create puzzle prizes to give to the winners. Ask students to determine how the solving of puzzles is related to a search for patterns and structures in the subject of mathematics.

Language Arts: READING

From the library, collect picture books about the environment similar to the book *Welcome to the Green House* written by Jane Yolen and illustrated by Laura Regan (published by G. P. Putnam's Sons of New York). Read these books and note the beautiful language patterns and colorful pictures that are used to send "earthy" messages and images to the reader. Develop an annotated bibliography of these books and write a series of reviews to promote these books to younger readers.

Study Skills: RESEARCH

Research to find out what historians refer to as the "seven wonders of the world." Construct a chart of their names, locations, ages, and physical features. Use this as a model for identifying your own "seven wonders" list of unique people, places, or things related to the environment. Some ideas for you to consider are:

- Seven Wonders of the Planet Earth
- Seven Wonders of the Desert
- Seven Wonders of the Animal World
- Seven Wonders of the Ecological World
- Seven Wonders of the Plant World
- Seven Wonders of Man-Made Environments
- Seven Wonders of the Grasslands
- Seven Wonders of Recycled Products
- Seven Wonders of the Rain Forest
- Seven Wonders of the Natural World

Language Arts: WRITING

Write a short ecological essay with the title: "Random Acts of Kindness and Senseless Beauty." What will your essay be about? Where will you find information for your essay? What themes will run through your essay? What examples can you give in your essay?

Ways To Make Every Day Earth Day

CONTENT-BASED ACTIVITIES

Science

Create a "Calendar-For-A-Day" calendar that contains a page for each school day and that provides an important fact, statistic, detail, concept, word, or quotation related to the environment. If possible, create a simple graphic or border for each page that reflects an environmental theme. Make your calendar for a week, month, or year depending upon the "kid power" you have available for this purpose. Perhaps you could produce these calendars in large quantities and sell them in the school or local book store to raise money for an environmental project.

Math/Science

Compile a list of number facts and statistics about the environment and/or creatures that make up the environment. Use these to construct a series of word problems to solve with your friends. Two examples are given here to get you started.

Problem: Snails are slow creatures that move just 10 to 12 feet per hour. On the other hand, the bamboo plant is very fast; it can grow as much as 36 inches in one day. How far would a snail travel in one week as compared with the traveling growth of the bamboo plant in that same period of time?

Problem: It is predicted that disposable diapers will make up five percent of the landfill waste by the year 2000. If there are 10,000 landfills in the U. S., how many landfills would disposable diapers fill during that time period?

Optional Extension

Work with a group of five other students from your class to read and write about the environmental issues listed below which are problems in most communities throughout the United States. To complete this task, have each student in the group take ten 4" x 6" file cards and write one of the issues on each card.

Each group member is to conduct independent research in the media center on each topic and is to record his or her own facts on the appropriate card. When all research has been completed, your group is to combine the ideas on the cards for each issue and use this information to write a group report of 12 paragraphs—an introductory paragraph, a paragraph about each issue, and a concluding paragraph.

Environmental Issues To Consider

1. Acid rain
2. Animal rights
3. Disposal of toxic wastes
4. Global warming
5. Destruction of the rain forest
6. Solid waste disposal
7. Noise pollution
8. Poor land use and abuse
9. Litter
10. Water conservation

Ways To Make Every Day Earth Day

— JOURNALING —

"We are all in this together."
"Reuse, Recycle, Refuse"
"Think globally, act locally."

Think about how these quotations apply to the environment and then write about your own responsibility for preserving the earth's natural resources for future generations. Write about what you can do today to contribute to a healthier, cleaner, and safer environment.

_____

_____

_____

_____

_____

_____

_____

_____

_____

_____

_____

_____

_____

_____

_____

_____

_____

_____

_____

_____

_____

_____

MINI
INTERDISCIPLINARY
THEMATIC
UNITS

Say What You Mean And Mean What You Say

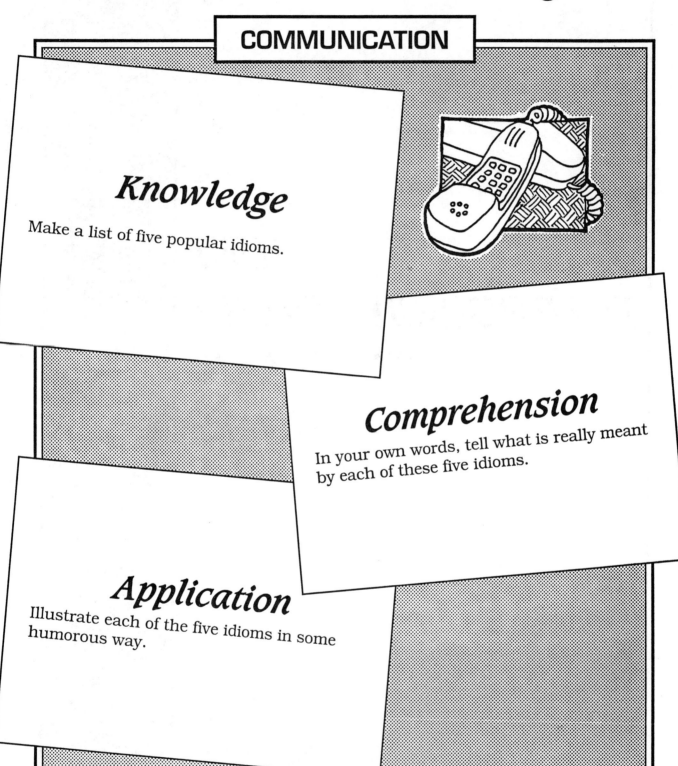

Knowledge

Make a list of five popular idioms.

Comprehension

In your own words, tell what is really meant by each of these five idioms.

Application

Illustrate each of the five idioms in some humorous way.

Say What You Mean And Mean What You Say

COMMUNICATION

Analysis

Choose any of the five idioms and infer how it came into existence.

Synthesis

Create a skit whose title and theme reflect one of the five idioms.

Evaluation

Rank order the idioms from one to five with one being your favorite and five being your least favorite. Give reasons for both your first and last choice.

Write Your Way Out

Fluency

List all of the occasions you can think of when someone might sit down and write a note or letter to another person.

Flexibility

Organize your "fluency" list in some logical way.

Originality

What is the most unusual or novel occasion you can think of for writing a note or letter to another person? Be original in your response.

Risk-Taking

Write a note or letter to yourself that honestly criticizes you in some way.

Write Your Way Out

Elaboration

Discuss the many advantages of sending a note or letter to someone you care about or haven't seen for a long time rather than making a telephone call to communicate.

Complexity

Explain how a letter might be considered a "gift."

Curiosity

What do you think a letter might say to each of the following: postage stamp, mailbox, glue manufacturer, and ball point pen.

Imagination

Imagine that you were to receive a special delivery letter from a famous celebrity. Whom would you want to hear from and what sorts of things would you want him or her to tell you about?

A Body Speaks
Louder Than Words

COMMUNICATION

Knowledge
Recite the rules for playing two popular games that do not require communication through the use of words: Charades and Pictionary.

Comprehension
In your own words, explain why these two games are popular with both kids and adults.

Application
Put together a list of book titles, characters, and plots that would lend themselves to the playing of either Charades or Pictionary. Use these to construct and play a game of Charades or Pictionary.

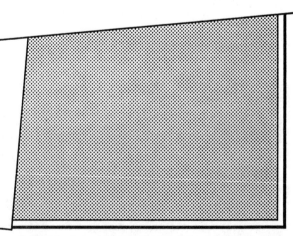

A Body Speaks Louder Than Words

Analysis

What special skills, interests, or aptitudes are most desirable in a partner or team member when playing either Charades or Pictionary?

Synthesis

Create a new television show for kids based on the gaming format of either Charades or Pictionary. Advertise your show in a one-minute commercial.

Evaluation

Which is more vivid and powerful—verbal or nonverbal communication? Defend your answer.

Kids And Gangs

Fluency

List all of the reasons you can think of that kids would want to belong to a gang.

Flexibility

Write down all of the reasons you can think of why kids would not want to be associated with a gang.

Originality

Determine the most unusual and unique criteria you can think of that would determine membership in a gang.

Elaboration

Defend or negate this statement about gangs: "Groups, such as gangs, form mainly to provide protection for each other whenever they are legitimately threatened."

Kids And Gangs

Risk-Taking

Describe the factors that would most interest you in becoming a gang member or continuing to be a gang member (if you are already a member of a gang).

Complexity

Explain why the appearance of graffiti is often one of the first signs of gang activity in a particular school or area of town.

Curiosity

Generate a set of interview questions you would like to ask a member of a well-known gang in a large urban city or a small suburban community.

Imagination

Imagine that you have been asked to join a citizen's group to "ungang" a community. Develop a plan for reducing and/or eliminating a gang's influences in this community.

Moods And Masks

Knowledge

Define the words "mood" and "emotion." List as many words as you can think of that would be classified as a mood or as an emotion.

Comprehension

Choose one or more of the mood or emotion words from your "knowledge" list and tell about a time when you experienced that mood or emotion.

Application

Browse through a series of magazines and cut out as many different pictures as you can find that portray people of various moods or that show faces of various emotions. Arrange these in an artistic collage, mount and frame the collage in some way, and give the collage an elaborate title. Use your collage to begin a "mood wall" of displays for your classroom.

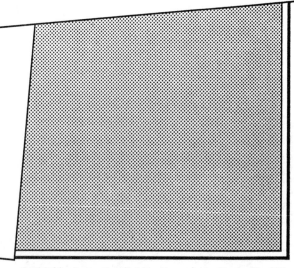

Moods And Masks

Analysis

Analyze your list of mood or emotion words from your "knowledge" list and arrange them according to some organizational scheme that reflects the intensity and range of their meanings. Fill in any gaps that are missing. For example, consider the connotations of such similar words as "happy," "jubilant," and "ecstatic." How do they vary in their intensity?

Synthesis

Choose a mood or emotion and design a mask from a paper plate mounted on a tongue depressor to reflect that mood. Create a short essay or story about the mood that is expressed by your mask.

Evaluation

Often different colors have been associated with different moods. Assume that each of the following moods is represented by one of the following colors. Match up each mood with a specific color and justify your match-ups through personal examples and observations.

Mood Choices: Joy, Anger, Excitement, Anticipation, Contentment, Sadness, Uneasiness, and Calmness.

Color Choices: Brown, Blue, Purple, Green, Yellow, Violet, Red, and Orange

Reading For Information

Knowledge

List all of the different resources available in the media center for obtaining information about any topic of your choice.

Comprehension

In your own words, explain why the late 20th century is considered to be the Information Age.

Application

Select a topic of interest to you and find information about it using any three resources from your "knowledge" list. Compile a fact sheet on the topic citing the specific source of each piece of information.

Reading
For Information

Analysis
Construct a chart comparing and contrasting each of the information sources from your "knowledge" list.

Synthesis
Compose an original news story warning people about the dangers of "information pollution" in today's society.

Evaluation
Of all the resources you listed, which one is the most versatile and useful to kids your age? Be able to defend your choice.

Magazines As Springboards For Personal Writing

COMMUNICATION

Fluency

List as many magazine titles as you can think of in three minutes.

Flexibility

Group or cluster your magazine titles in some way. Add other titles to your list to fill in any gaps in your classification schemata. Put an asterisk next to each magazine title that uses lots of photographs or pictures to illustrate its articles.

Originality

Make up a magazine title and a list of special features for a magazine that hasn't been invented yet. Try writing a "mock-up" of its first issue. Make certain that your magazine has a special theme for a given content area.

Elaboration

Choose a favorite magazine (or group of magazines) from your list. Cut out and mount at least 10 pictures from the magazine(s). Use these pictures to complete the following tasks and to elaborate on each picture's theme.
1. Compare and contrast any two pictures.
2. Write a creative caption for one picture and five phrases to describe what is happening.
3. Choose a picture and tell what you think will happen next.
4. Write a series of riddles based on a picture of your choice.
5. Make up a short story using some of the pictures in your collection.
6. Select a picture that illustrates one or more familiar proverbs such as: "Action speaks louder than words" or "Birds of a feather flock together."

Magazines As Springboards For Personal Writing

COMMUNICATION

Risk-Taking

Select a picture that makes you feel happy, peaceful, angry, confused, or sad. Use words to explain why you feel as you do.

Curiosity

If you could interview a famous photographer for a popular magazine of your choice, what would you want to ask him or her?

Complexity

Find a picture you like in your collection and write a detailed description of it. Give your written description to a friend and see if he or she can recreate the picture by drawing it according to your description.

Imagination

Pretend you are a famous editor of a prize-winning magazine and are about to receive the country's annual Publisher Award. Describe how you feel at this moment by writing a metaphor to express yourself.

Impromptu Speaking

Knowledge

Use the dictionary to define "impromptu."
What is an impromptu speech?

Comprehension

In your own words, discuss times when people might be either inclined or forced to give an impromptu speech.

Application

With a group of friends, think of 30 topics for an impromptu speech and write each one on a separate strip of paper. Put these topics in a container and take turns drawing them out to give an impromptu speech of 45 seconds to one minute.

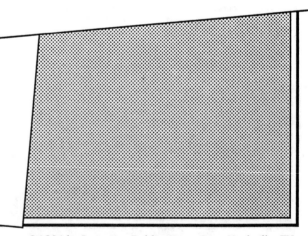

98

Impromptu Speaking

Analysis

What types of topics are easiest or most difficult for you to talk about in giving an impromptu speech? Give reasons for your answers.

Synthesis

Give an informal speech about a time when you were "speechless" because of something that happened.

Evaluation

What advice would you give to someone who is about to give an impromptu speech?

Poetry Figures

Knowledge

Define each of the following poetry terms and put them into a glossary format: pun, personification, simile, idiom, onomatopoeia, hyperbole, alliteration, and metaphor.

Comprehension

Explain how figures of speech are used to enrich one's personal reading and writing. Show illustrations from favorite poems to support your response.

Application

Browse through a poetry book and find examples of each of the poetry terms listed in the "knowledge" section. Record your examples on a set of file cards so that you have each term on a separate card. Try to find examples that represent many different poetry themes, topics, or subjects. Show how poetry is a communication form that crosses many diverse content areas.

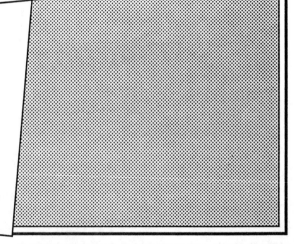

Poetry Figures

Analysis

Make inferences about what types of poems or poets are most appealing to students in your class. Compile a collection of diverse poems and poets on an audio tape or in a booklet form and survey students in your class to determine their favorites. Graph the results and compare with your initial inferences about personal preferences.

Synthesis

Create a poetry anthology on a particular theme such as food, conflict, nature, humor, or sea creatures. Copy your collection of poems in a notebook, on a poster, or as part of a collage. Illustrate each poem.

Evaluation

Work with a small group of peers and suggest that each of you develop a new and original form of poetry by writing each set of your rules on a piece of paper. Your rules can be as serious or as funny as you like. Consider this set of rules as an example:

Line 1: Use a word ending in "est."
Line 2: Use three words that name hide-aways.
Line 3: Use three words ending in "ing" to describe Line 2.
Line 4: Use five words as a personal quote.
Line 5: Use a word ending in "est."
Your poem might read something like this:

Greatest
Treehouse, cave, beach
Retreating, relaxing, dreaming
A place all my own
Happiest

Share your original poetry forms with one another and try creating original poems by following one another's rules. Decide which poetry form is best and defend your decision.

Play It Safe!

Fluency

In five minutes, brainstorm as many school policies, procedures, and physical features as you can that exist to protect the safety of students.

Flexibility

Classify the items in your "fluency" list, and explain your classification scheme.

Originality

Think of a new and unique safety policy, procedure, or physical feature for your school and design a flyer, poster, or display ad to promote it.

Elaboration

The results: cracked walls, broken glass, and frightened kids. What do you think happened?

Play It Safe!

Risk-Taking

Explain what would be the most difficult thing for you to do if you had to administer first aid, CPR, or the Heimlich maneuver on someone in a school emergency.

Complexity

Which would be the most difficult health hazard for you to deal with personally in school: sexual abuse, physical abuse, or emotional abuse? Explain.

Curiosity

What causes one person to abuse or hurt another?

Imagination

Visualize a school setting with no vandalism, theft, conflict, or threats. What would it look like, feel like, and sound like?

The Transition Gap

Knowledge

The dictionary defines "transition" as "an act, process, or instance of changing from one state, form, activity, or place to another." Record a use of the term "transition" from your science class or textbook.

Comprehension

In your own words, explain the meaning of "transition" as it relates to your own growth and development at home, at school, or in the community.

Application

Construct a chart showing the transitional stages for your life (past, present, and future) and the transitional stages of life for some other creature representative of the animal world.

The Transition Gap

Analysis

Debate the validity of this transition-related statement by Ivy Baker Priest: "The world is round and the place which may seem like the end may also be only the beginning."

Synthesis

Invent a scientific or visual symbol to represent the concept of "transition" as you understand it.

Evaluation

Determine what makes a "transition" period easy or difficult for someone going through it.

What Makes You Tick?

Knowledge

Define the word "environment" and list the features that would make up a good classroom environment for learning.

Comprehension

In your own words, explain what you think is meant by the "ecology of the classroom."

Application

Collect information about the needed resources for maintaining a quality science program for your school.

What Makes You Tick?

Analysis

We often talk about the importance of maintaining a balance in nature. How can we apply this notion to maintaining a balance of learning modalities (auditory, visual, and tactile activities) in the classroom?

Synthesis

Visualize all of the ways that a classroom is like a desert, a rain forest, a tundra, or a grassland.

Evaluation

Determine ways that individuals can and do pollute the environment of the classroom so that growth and development of students is limited.

Alternative Ways To Measure School Pride, Spirit, Or Culture

SCHOOL CULTURE AND ACADEMIC SURVIVAL

Knowledge

Define the following terms which can be used in the process of evaluating something:
- survey
- questionnaire
- checklist
- interview
- observation

Comprehension

Explain why and how the evaluation tools listed in the "knowledge" section might be used to measure the pride, spirit, or culture of a school.

Application

Prepare a survey, questionnaire, checklist, interview, and observation instrument that could be used to measure your school pride, spirit, or culture. What questions will you ask? What criteria or evidence will you look for? What format will you use? What rating scale will you decide on?

Alternative Ways To Measure School Pride, Spirit, Or Culture

SCHOOL CULTURE AND ACADEMIC SURVIVAL

Analysis

Construct a chart and compare and contrast each of these evaluation tools with one another. How are they alike and how are they different? What are the advantages and disadvantages of using each type of instrument in the evaluation process?

Synthesis

Administer your survey from the "application" section and compile the results in some creative and unusual way. Develop a plan for improving one significant area of weakness.

Evaluation

Rate the effectiveness of each of your evaluation tools. Which ones generated the best data? How do you know?

Tangrams

Knowledge

Define tangrams and identify their origin.

Comprehension

Describe the many different ways that tangrams can be used as a learning tool in the classroom.

Application

Construct a set of tangrams out of cardboard and use these to develop a set of tangram puzzles for others to figure out.

Tangrams

Analysis

Determine why tangrams are so popular with both children and adults.

Synthesis

Create an unusual shape with your set of tangrams. Write equivalent mathematical statements on each pair of matching edges (or portions of edges) of the puzzle pieces so that the shape can only be put together correctly by matching the appropriate equivalent edges.

Evaluation

Defend or negate this statement: The use of tangrams can reinforce logical thinking in the area of mathematics.

The Round World
Of Circles

Fluency

List all of the things you can think of that are circular or made of circles.

Flexibility

Think of additional things that are extensions of circles such as spheres, cylinders, and cones.

Originality

What is the most unusual and unique type of circle that you can think of? For example, hugs are circles with your arms and whistles are circles with your lips.

Elaboration

Explain why circles are amazing or special and yet often mysterious shapes as well.

The Round World
Of Circles

Risk-Taking

Tell about a time when you were so frustrated that you were "running around in circles."

Complexity

Explain why King Arthur sat at a round table with his knights rather than at a square or rectangular table.

Curiosity

Think of some questions you would like to ask Viking or Zulu architects of ancient times who built "round towns" for their people.

Imagination

Fantasize what it would be like to be completely circle shaped so that you would just roll over and over rather than walk upright with a head, arms, and feet.

Organize A Visitor's Bureau For Your School

SCHOOL CULTURE AND ACADEMIC SURVIVAL

Knowledge

List all of the different types of visitors who are likely to come to your school on any given day. Organize your list in some meaningful way.

Comprehension

In your own words, describe how your school would appear to a typical visitor. Consider visitor procedures, policies, invitations, challenges, activities, and perceptions.

Application

With a group of your classmates, keep a record of all the visitors who come to the school office on a specific day as well as reasons for those visits. Graph your results.

Organize A Visitor's Bureau For Your School

Analysis

Survey the visitors who come to the school office and form generalizations about how well they were treated and/or how satisfied they were with the outcome of their visits.

Synthesis

Create a "Visitor's Bureau" for your school that will help visitors feel more welcome and that will help facilitate the purpose of their visit.

Evaluation

Design a way to evaluate the success of your "Visitor's Bureau." Has it made a difference in the way visitors are treated at your school?

Attending To Business

Fluency

Make a list of as many reasons as you can think of that a school might have a good attendance record or a poor attendance record.

Flexibility

Group the reasons in both of your lists from the "fluency" section in some way that makes sense to you.

Originality

What is the most original excuse or reason you can think of for not attending school?

Elaboration

Analyze the attendance records for your class and determine whether the attendance numbers are good or bad. What criteria will you use to make that determination? Explain your rationale.

Attending To Business

Risk-Taking

What event would make you choose to "skip" school on an important day?

Complexity

Discuss things a school might do to improve its attendance records or truancy rates?

Curiosity

What would happen if kids could "drop in and out of school" whenever they wanted?

Imagination

Visualize a school that did not take attendance but depended on the honor system to chart a student's attendance record. How do you think it would function? How could you make it work to the benefit of all parties involved?

Designing The Perfect Parent/Teacher Conference

Knowledge

Recall a time when your parents and teacher(s) had a conference about you. How did it go?

Comprehension

Explain why you think parent/teacher conferences are more or less informative about how a student is doing in class or in school than a report card is likely to be.

Application

With a friend plan and act out a simulated parent/teacher conference that you would consider to be effective. Do the same thing in which the outcome would be a disaster. What accounts for the difference?

Designing The Perfect Parent/Teacher Conference

SCHOOL CULTURE AND ACADEMIC SURVIVAL

Analysis

Compare and contrast the benefits of quarterly parent/teacher conferences with quarterly written reports to assess student academic progress.

Synthesis

Design a report card that could be used to rate parent and/or teacher behavior at a conference. What grading, ranking, or assessment scale will you use for this purpose?

Evaluation

Defend or negate this idea: Regular parent conferences should replace report cards as the primary method for assessing a student's progress in school.

We're All In This Together

Knowledge
List as many different ethnic or cultural groups as you can think of.

Comprehension
Explain what the words "culture" and "ethnicity" mean and how they are related.

Application
Interview someone with a different culture or ethnic background from you. Write out your interview questions and the results of the interview process.

We're All In This Together

Analysis

Survey members of the class to determine what prejudices or stereotypes they have commonly associated with different ethnic or cultural groups. Infer how these might have evolved.

Synthesis

Produce a small skit, role play, or case study to teach others in the class something about cultural diversity.

Evaluation

Which of these activities do you think would be most helpful for someone to pursue if they wanted to learn more about a different culture: reading and research in the media center, personal interviews and observations, visitations to the home or workplace, student exchange programs, or discussion sessions? Justify your decision.

Parents As People

Knowledge

What is the perfect age for a parent or legal guardian to be? How do you know?

Comprehension

Describe how your parents (guardians) treat you and how they show their pride in you.

Application

Compile a set of "Dos and Don'ts For Kids" on how to get along with their parents.

Parents As People

Analysis

If you could tell all the parents in the world three things to help them get along better with their kids, what three things would you tell them?

Synthesis

Design a special "Parent Lounge" for your school.

Evaluation

The rate of unwanted teenage pregnancies is increasing at an alarming rate. Decide what factors are contributing to this problem and what can be done about it. Support your ideas with facts.

As Time Goes By

Fluency

List as many excuses as you can for being late to school.

Flexibility

Think of ten good uses for a broken watch.

Originality

Prepare a one-minute speech on this topic:

"Timely Tips For _____."

Elaboration

Describe an alarm clock to someone who has never seen or used one.

As Time Goes By

Risk-Taking

Write a short paragraph telling the teacher how you "waste time" in class.

Complexity

Explain how and why time is a natural resource.

Curiosity

What kinds of things improve with age or time?

Imagination

Imagine what a sun dial might say to an egg timer, a grandfather clock, or a stop watch.

Teamwork Is No Mystery To The Science World

SELF-CONCEPT AND RELATIONSHIPS

Knowledge

If you were putting together an important team to conduct a special scientific expedition, list the desirable characteristics you would want in all of your team members.

Comprehension

In your own words, summarize the differences between being a member in a science group and being a member of a science team.

Application

It has been said that a successful team in science or any other subject must go through five developmental stages in order to function and complete the assigned task. Each of these stages has its own set of behaviors or characteristics. Construct a chart to show what you think team members are like when they go through each of the following stages:
- FORMING STAGE
- STORMING STAGE
- NORMING STAGE
- PERFORMING STAGE
- ADJOURNING STAGE

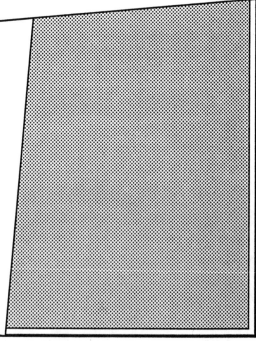

Teamwork Is No Mystery
To The Science World

SELF-CONCEPT AND RELATIONSHIPS

Analysis

Compare and contrast a team of scientists with a team of baseball players. How might they be alike and how might they be different?

Synthesis

Pretend you are putting together a team of science students to compete in a national science fair team competition. Describe the type of science project you would like to complete and the people on your science team that would be important to this project's success.

Evaluation

Develop an evaluation form or checklist that could be used to assess the results of your group's performance and project.

A Career As A Scientist

Fluency

List as many science-related careers as you can think of in three minutes.

Flexibility

Classify this list of science-related careers in as many different ways as you can.

Originality

Think of an unusual or unique science-related career of the future that doesn't exist at this time but that is likely to be a reality by the year 2050.

Elaboration

Add to this starter statement: "The most important scientific discovery of the last century was . . . because . . ."

A Career As A Scientist

SELF-CONCEPT AND RELATIONSHIPS

Risk-Taking

Generate a list of reasons why you would or would not be a good candidate for a science-related career.

Complexity

Discuss the implications of this thought about the world of work: "Work is not something we have to do. It is something we have the opportunity to do that adds depth and texture to our lives."

Curiosity

Write down a series of "wonder statements" in the area of science about which you are curious to know more. Then choose one of the items to research. Examples: I wonder how homing pigeons find their way home.
I wonder how the path of a hurricane is predicted.
I wonder how the speed of a fastball is measured.
I wonder how truth serum works.
I wonder how snakes are charmed.
I wonder how dry ice is made.
I wonder how a corpse is embalmed.

Imagination

Imagine that you have been selected to receive this year's Nobel Prize in Science. Describe what you have done and why it is so important to the rest of the world.

Enjoying My Social Self Through Science

SELF-CONCEPT AND RELATIONSHIPS

Knowledge

It is your birthday and you are to plan a party for yourself with a science theme. Write down as many science-related topics as you can think of that might lend themselves to a birthday party event. Record them in alphabetical order.

Comprehension

Select one of the topics from your "knowledge" list as your birthday theme and describe what famous science celebrities (living or dead) you would like to invite to your party and why they were chosen for this honor.

Application

Construct a birthday invitation that you could send out to both your own personal friends and your science celebrity friends. Complete a list of theme-related party favors and decorations that will also be used for this gala event.

Enjoying My Social Self Through Science

SELF-CONCEPT AND RELATIONSHIPS

Analysis

Determine whether or not you think a birthday party with a science-related theme is more likely to be a success than a birthday party with no theme at all.

Synthesis

Create a series of special science-related games and events that you could play or do at your birthday party. Create your own birthday cake design as well as a gift paper motif for wrapping the party prizes and favors.

Evaluation

Devise a plan for determining whether your birthday party was a success or not and what you would do differently if you were to have it over again. What criteria will you use in this assessment process?

Kids Can Do Their Share

SELF-CONCEPT AND RELATIONSHIPS

Fluency

Look through the Yellow Pages and write down as many groups or organizations that you can think of or find that provide services for the homeless, handicapped, helpless, abused, ill, underprivileged, victimized, or indigent.

Flexibility

List all the different reasons why individuals and families find themselves seeking help from volunteer organizations and services such as those from your "fluency" list. Can you categorize these in some meaningful way?

Originality

Describe the most unusual and unique organization you discovered that provides a service to those in need.

Elaboration

Decide which of the following community service projects would be of interest to you and develop a detailed plan to pursue it in your community.
1. Plant and care for a food garden.
2. Organize a Saturday Reading Club and Library for kids in a homeless shelter.
3. Conduct an art program for a nursing home.
4. Record histories of senior citizens for their families.
5. Adopt a grandparent.
6. Open a tutoring service for underprivileged students.
7. Form a birthday club for a group of people in a housing project.
8. Raise money for an organization by holding a raffle, staging a marathon, putting on a play or concert, holding a toy drive, or hosting a potluck dinner.

Kids Can Do Their Share

SELF-CONCEPT AND RELATIONSHIPS

Risk-Taking
Tell how you would feel if the government passed a law that forced every family to exchange homes with a family from a homeless shelter for one week to see "how the other half lives."

Complexity
Speculate as to why the number of children living in poverty in the U.S. has dropped 17 percent since 1960, but has increased 40 percent since 1970.

Curiosity
If you were to interview a victim of alcoholism, abuse, or poverty what things would you want to know?

Imagination
Imagine how your community would be different if all people had jobs to earn a living, enough food to eat, and homes of their own. What would it be like?

It's All In The Cards

Knowledge

Make a list of all the card games you and a group of friends can think of that are played with a deck of 52 cards.

Comprehension

In your own words, explain the unique meaning of these terms as they relate to a game of cards: bluff, book, draw, face card, face down, suit, hand, layout, lead, round, sequence, singleton, trick, trump, and wild card.

Application

Obtain a book of card games for kids from the library and use it to learn how to play one of the following games (or make up your own rules for playing the game):
1. Snap
2. Give Away
3. Chase the Ace
4. Pyramid
5. Comet
6. Catch the Ten
7. Sevens
8. Play or Pay
9. Go Boom
10. Tricks

It's All In The Cards

Analysis

Look over your list of card games from the "knowledge" section and analyze the different strategies or ways cards can be used in a game.

Synthesis

Create a trivia game using "jacks, kings, and queens" as the theme. Develop a set of questions whose answer is a famous jack, king, or queen. Example: What is an important city in the state of New York? Answer: Queenstown; What is the scientific name for a type of wild dog that lives in Africa, Asia, and parts of eastern Europe? Answer: jackal; Who is a famous female tennis player whose first name sounds like a boy's name? Answer: Billie Jean King

Evaluation

Did you know that the design of playing cards is considered a form of art? They are currently manufactured in all different colors and with many varied graphics on them. Many years ago, kids would collect playing cards as a hobby and would trade them with one another much as they do baseball cards today. Likewise, decks of playing cards have also been modified for classroom use to teach important science, math, or social studies concepts. For example, decks of cards with pictures and facts about U.S. presidents, endangered species, and optical illusions are sold as learning tools in the schools. Students can play any of the traditional card games and learn subject matter at the same time, or they can invent new card games that capitalize on the information presented. Stage a contest for the other students in your class to create the most popular artistic and/or instructional design for playing cards that have a special appeal or purpose for kids. Establish a set of criteria for judging the designs and give reasons for your first, second, and third place choices.

Learning To Be Peacemakers

Fluency

Brainstorm all the different types of situations which cause conflict among kids your age.

Flexibility

Classify your list of potential conflict situations from the "fluency" section according to when and where they are most likely to occur or according to conflict sources.

Originality

Make up a conflict situation. Then ask for a small group of your friends to volunteer to act out your original conflict but stopping the role play before these student actors have resolved their problem. Then ask other small groups of peers to identify the conflict and act out alternative solutions.

Elaboration

Add details to the following conflict scenario including its potential outcome:
"While waiting at the school bus stop one morning, Dan, an 8th grader, grabs the lunch money from Jeremy, a 6th grader, and refuses to give it back."

Learning To Be Peacemakers

SELF-CONCEPT AND RELATIONSHIPS

Risk-Taking

Pretend you have been assigned the job of serving as a "peace mediator" in your classroom, a new program that recruits and trains student volunteers to help solve their own daily conflicts. You have been taught the six steps in the mediation process: (1) open the session; (2) gather the information; (3) focus on interests and perceptions; (4) create optional solutions; (5) decide on solutions; and (6) seek agreement. Describe what you think should be done during each of these steps and how you would feel about serving in this role to settle disputes among your peers.

Curiosity

Have you ever wondered what a conflict looks like from another person's point of view? Try role-playing a conflict situation that you have recently experienced in your own life. Do this with a friend. After you finish the role play, try switching roles and acting out the situation again from the other person's perspective. What did you experience in this role reversal?

Complexity

Prove that conflict is an important part of growing up.

Imagination

Fantasize yourself as the character in a popular book that presents a conflict such as *The Bully of Barkham Street* by Mary Stolz (Harper Collins, 1985). What kinds of things would you do or not do in this story?

Crack The Code

Knowledge

Define "code" and "cipher."

Comprehension

Collect information about each of the following types of codes: Morse Code, Braille, sign language, flag signals, and number codes. Explain how these codes are used in the workplace.

Application

Practice using one of the codes from the "comprehension" section to communicate with a friend.

Crack The Code

Analysis

Compare and contrast any two of the codes from the "comprehension" section.

Synthesis

Invent a number code of your own. Send messages to your friends and teachers using your code. How can you help them "crack" the code in order to use it?

Evaluation

Determine which of the codes from the "comprehension" section would be most difficult for you to learn. Why?

What Can The Comics Teach Us About Individual Choices And Group Membership?

PROBLEM-SOLVING AND DECISION-MAKING

Knowledge

Comic strip characters come in all sizes, sexes, shapes, and ages. List as many of these characters as you can think of as well as adjectives to describe each one's basic personality and behavior patterns.

Comprehension

Describe how comic strips tend to chronicle or reflect real people, places, and events in our society over time.

Application

Locate a comic strip whose characters and plotline provide the reader with:
- an example of a stereotype
- an example of a conflict
- an example of a human value
- an example of a prejudice
- an example of a social problem
- an example of a family or work crisis
- an example of a cause-and-effect relationship

What Can The Comics Teach Us About Individual Choices And Group Membership?

PROBLEM-SOLVING AND DECISION-MAKING

Analysis

Study the comic strips to determine the degree to which they reflect our current American lifestyle.

Synthesis

Compose a short essay about why you would like to assume the identity of a particular comic strip character.

Evaluation

Develop a rating scale for evaluating the violence and/or negative influences of comic strips on children that is similar to the one used for motion pictures or the one proposed for cartoons and television shows.

The Nutritious Orange

PROBLEM-SOLVING AND DECISION-MAKING

Fluency

List the many attributes of an orange.

Flexibility

Think of twenty-five varied things that are the color of an orange. Group them in some meaningful way.

Originality

Construct a puppet in the shape of an orange. Create a clever skit or play about the uniqueness of an orange in which your puppet will star.

Elaboration

Expand on this statement: "An orange is more versatile than an apple because . . ."

The Nutritious Orange

PROBLEM-SOLVING AND DECISION-MAKING

Risk-Taking

Experiment to discover the three best ways to prepare and serve an orange. Convince others to think as you do.

Complexity

Discuss ways the taste, texture, nutritious value, and color of an orange could be improved.

Curiosity

Make a list of things you would like to know about the process for commercially producing orange juice from an orange.

Imagination

Fantasize about what life would be like if everything were colored orange or tasted like an orange. What unusual effects would this have?

Ads Add Up When It Comes To Health And Hygiene

PROBLEM-SOLVING AND DECISION-MAKING

Fluency

List or find all of the health, hygiene, and grooming products you can think of in five minutes that are advertised in magazines you read or television commercials you watch. You may look through old magazines to help you with this task.

Flexibility

Classify these products according to the type of advertising strategy that seems to work best for them. Consider such strategies as: Bandwagon, Testimonial, Scientific Words/Facts, Celebrity Endorsement, Before and After Scenes, Card Stacking (stressing good points of one product over another), Sex Appeal, Statistics, or Symbols/Logos/Animated Figures.

Originality

Describe the most unusual and unique advertising jingle or slogan you can think of that promotes a health, hygiene, or grooming product.

Elaboration

Elaborate on this idea: "Advertising and promotional methods are designed only to create greater demands for a product or service even among customers who don't need them."

Ads Add Up When It Comes To Health And Hygiene

PROBLEM-SOLVING AND DECISION-MAKING

Risk-Taking

Describe how you would tell someone you know and care about that they have an "odor problem" or a "dandruff" problem. Explain how you would react if a friend said the same thing to you.

Complexity

Summarize ways that personal motives and values affect consumer decisions.

Curiosity

Write down a list of questions you would like to ask the manufacturer of your favorite mouthwash, toothpaste, or breath freshener.

Imagination

Visualize yourself as a member of a local department store's Teen Board for promoting good grooming and hygiene habits for teenagers. Create a Top Ten list of "must" products and practices that you would advocate for kids your age.

Let's Get Physical

Knowledge

Record ways that you and your friends work at being physically fit. Put a circle around the most popular activities among your peers.

Comprehension

Describe an ideal exercise program for kids your age. Be specific in your recommendations.

Application

Work with the physical education teachers in your school to create an obstacle course on the school grounds to challenge one's fitness and physical stamina. Construct a checklist of warm-up exercises for students to do before taking on the challenge of the obstacle course. Use your ideas from the "comprehension" section for this purpose.

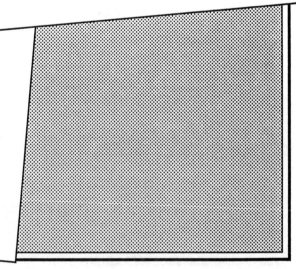

Let's Get Physical

PROBLEM-SOLVING AND DECISION-MAKING

Analysis

Determine what part of the United States is most likely to promote and produce kids who are physically fit.

Synthesis

Health clubs are becoming more and more popular with adults today especially in big cities and in cold climates. Design a health club for kids that is creative, challenging, and child-centered. Create a brochure that describes its facilities and programs.

Evaluation

Assess how television limits the physical activity of children in the home today as compared to a generation ago.

Group Choices And Their Effects On Individuals

Fluency

List as many reasons as you can think of for supermarkets to offer only paper bags to their customers for packing their groceries.

Flexibility

List as many reasons as you can think of for supermarkets to offer only plastic bags to their customers for packing their groceries.

Originality

Write down the most unusual and unique thing you can think of to make with a collection of recycled paper or plastic bags.

Elaboration

Defend or negate this statement: "Shoppers should have to bring reusable cloth bags to carry their goods home from the supermarket or they will not be able to purchase any products."

Group Choices And Their Effects On Individuals

PROBLEM-SOLVING AND DECISION-MAKING

Risk-Taking

List the ways you waste paper products in your home and at school.

Complexity

It has been said by foreigners that America is a "throw-away" society. Explain the logic behind this perception.

Curiosity

In European countries, the majority of consumers choose to do their shopping on a daily (rather than a weekly) basis, and they always use canvas bags for this purpose. If you could interview one of these European family members, what questions would you want to ask them about this habit?

Imagination

Imagine that you have been commissioned by the National Association of Supermarket Managers to create the ultimate canvas shopping bag for American consumers to use for their future purchases. Design what it would look like and draw your bag according to scale.

The World Of Advertising And Its Impact On You

Fluency

Brainstorm a list of as many advertising slogans, jingles, or logos as you can think of in five minutes.

Flexibility

Categorize your list of slogans, jingles, and logos from the "fluency" section according to whether the products and services they represent are also supported by scientific data or claims in their advertisements or commercials.

Originality

Think of an original slogan, jingle, or logo to replace one of those for a product or service listed in the "fluency" section. Try to give it a scientific twist.

Elaboration

In an average lifetime, the average American is hit with 136,692,500 advertisements and commercial messages. Of those, 18,549,172 are noticed and 2,925,220 are remembered. Infer what you think these figures tell us about the impact of advertising on the public.

The World Of Advertising And Its Impact On You

PROBLEM-SOLVING AND DECISION-MAKING

Risk-Taking

Create a short television commercial giving reasons why you think the opposite sex should be attracted to you.

Complexity

Describe how the quality of advertising would change if all advertisements and commercials had to be based on scientific facts and data.

Curiosity

Which would be more intriguing to you in the selling of a new product for teenagers: a billboard on the school grounds, an animated commercial over the school's public television station, or a full color ad in the school newspaper? Explain.

Imagination

Imagine you are the first child prodigy to serve as CEO (Chief Executive Officer) of a juvenile advertising agency. What excites you the most?

What Does Work Mean To A Scientist?

Knowledge

Write the scientific definition of "work" as it relates to the field of physics and as it refers to the study of energy.

Comprehension

In your own words, explain the meaning of work in each of the following contexts:

- What does "work" mean to a student in school?
- What does "work" mean to a football player?
- What does "work" mean to a carpenter?
- What does "work" mean to a movie actor/actress?
- What does "work" mean to a housewife?
- What does "work" mean to a stamp collector?
- What does "work" mean to a retiree?
- What does "work" mean to a robot?

Application

Create a series of mathematical word problems that reflect your definitions of "work" in each of the situations listed in the "comprehension" section. Solve the word problems and create an answer key.

What Does Work Mean To A Scientist?

PROBLEM-SOLVING AND DECISION-MAKING

Analysis

Research to find out how each of the following things work. Write your findings in a short report format.

1. How does a camera work?
2. How does an elevator work?
3. How does a photocopier work?
4. How does a piano work?
5. How does a digital watch work?
6. How does a refrigerator work?
7. How does a flashlight work?
8. How does a car engine work?

Synthesis

Create a cartoon character for a comic strip entitled: "The Workaholic." Draw its first comic strip story.

Evaluation

Construct an ABC list of occupations so that you have one type of work listed for each letter of the alphabet. Decide which three on the list require the most work from the worker. What criteria will you use and what reasons can you give to defend your choices?

Bubble Mania

Fluency

List all of the descriptive words (opaque), images (gliding through the air), metaphors (She has a bubbly personality), examples (bubbles in carbonated drinks), and inventions (bubble gum) you can think of related to the idea of "bubbles."

Flexibility

Think of the many ways you might use bubbles to teach a concept in different subject areas such as:

Math: Blow some bubbles and measure distances to where each is popped or predict number of bubbles produced by each blow.

Science: Research to find out what causes bubbles to form or where we are most likely to find bubbles in the environment.

Language Arts: Write a series of poems about bubbles or create a cartoon story complete with bubbles for recording the dialogue among characters.

Social Studies: Describe ways we have adapted the bubble to man-made objects such as a dome or head gear.

Originality

Experiment with different types of bubble mixtures that you can either make or buy to determine which solution produces the most unusual and unique bubbles.

Elaboration

Add details to this idea about bubbles: "A bubble is much like a balloon, a prism, and a kaleidoscope because . . ."

Bubble Mania

Risk-Taking

Tell about a time when you did something that made you behave like a "bubblehead."

Complexity

Give an explanation for where bubbles go when they break.

Curiosity

Make a list of things you would be curious to ask someone such as a deep sea diver or a glass blower about the importance of "bubbles" in their work.

Imagination

Visualize what it would be like to be a bubble floating in the air or a vacationer visiting a bubble city. Keep a diary of your observations and adventures.

LEARNING CENTERS

Making School History

PORTABLE DESK TOP FORMAT

— COMMUNICATION —

Activity One

You will be developing a data base of school trivia to share with others in your classroom. Work with a partner to choose a topic to investigate. Some ideas to think about might be:

1. How many incoming phone calls does the school office receive each day of the week? Which day is the busiest?

2. How many boxes of markers does the art teacher order each year?

3. How many dozens of cookies are baked in the school cafeteria each month?

4. How many packages of hand towels are purchased each year?

5. How many "lost and found" items are turned in at the end of each school day?

6. How many times is the typical student absent from school in a given school year?

7. What is the average report card grade for students in science, math, or physical education classes?

Making School History

PORTABLE DESK TOP FORMAT

— COMMUNICATION —

Activity Two

Design a "Guidebook for the First Week of School" directed to students new to your school. Some items to include in the guidebook might be:

- Staff directory
- Building floor plan
- School calendar marked with important dates
- List of school rules and policies
- Information about school hours and attendance procedures
- Outline of school colors, slogan, mascot
- Overview of school clubs and extracurricular activities
- Profile of student leaders

Making School History

COMMUNICATION

Activity Three

If you could redesign your school so that it would be ideal, how would you complete the following starter statements?

1. At the ideal school, no one has to . . .

2. At the ideal school, kids are allowed to . . .

3. At the ideal school, teachers always . . .

4. At the ideal school, the principal never . . .

5. At the ideal school, everyone learns how to . . .

6. At the ideal school, there are no . . .

7. At the ideal school, you get in trouble only when you . . .

8. At the ideal school, in the hall there are signs that read . . .

9. At the ideal school, parents can't . . .

10. At the ideal school, they pass out . . .

Making School History

PORTABLE DESK TOP FORMAT

— COMMUNICATION —

Activity Four

Pretend that you have been asked to prepare a time capsule which describes your school to people 100 years from now. Make a list of ten items you would want placed in the time capsule and give reasons for choosing each item.

ITEM

1. _____   6. _____
2. _____   7. _____
3. _____   8. _____
4. _____   9. _____
5. _____   10. _____

REASON FOR CHOOSING

1. _____
2. _____
3. _____
4. _____
5. _____
6. _____
7. _____
8. _____
9. _____
10. _____

Making School History

PORTABLE DESK TOP FORMAT

─── COMMUNICATION ───

Activity Five

Work with your classmates to compile a Class Almanac for this school year. Brainstorm a list of topics that you might want to include in your almanac. To help you get started, think of an almanac entry in each category suggested below.

1. Home remedy for illness
2. Silly horoscope for a month
3. Ecology tip
4. Local poem, story, or legend
5. Special proverb or saying
6. Synopsis of popular book
7. Best joke, riddle, or limerick
8. Challenging brain teaser
9. Famous birthday
10. Interview with school personnel
11. How-to craft
12. Favorite recipe

The Rewards Of Personal Listening

POCKET PACKET FORMAT

COMMUNICATION

Activity One

Think about how you and your family listen to one another. Do your parents or guardians listen attentively when you have something to say, or do they show little interest in what you are saying? Do other members of your family give you their complete attention when you are talking to them, or do they have a tendency to interrupt or "turn off" to what you are telling them? Analyze a typical family conversation time around a meal, an outing, or an evening without television. Record your observations and draw some conclusions about the listening habits of your family.

Activity Two

Use the ten items below to evaluate your own ability to listen at home, school, or in the community. Rate yourself on each item according to this scale:

> 1 = I do this all of the time.
> 2 = I do this most of the time.
> 3 = I do this some of the time.
> 4 = I do this none of the time.

1. Concentrate on what is being said even if I'm not interested
2. Tune people out who don't agree with me
3. Give the appearance of listening when I'm not
4. Let my mind wander while speaker is talking
5. Assume I know what speaker is going to say and stop listening
6. Look at the person who is speaking
7. Listen to only what I want to hear
8. Begin focusing on my thoughts of how to respond before speaker is finished talking
9. Clarify ideas presented by the speaker to enhance my understanding of what is being said
10. Listen to speaker without judging or criticizing

The Rewards Of Personal Listening

POCKET PACKET FORMAT

COMMUNICATION

Activity Three

Which of the following definitions of "listening" makes the most sense to you? Defend your position in a paragraph stating some personal examples and reflections.

1. Listening is a process in perpetual motion.

2. Listening is a two-way exchange in which all parties involved must be receptive to the thoughts, ideas, and emotions of others.

3. Listening is the accurate perception of what is being communicated.

4. Listening is a process that goes against human nature.

Activity Four

Share a personal experience that demonstrates how one of the advantages listed below becomes a very good reason to listen.

1. Listening keeps you out of trouble.

2. Listening tells you what is happening.

3. Listening makes you more competent.

4. Listening makes you look smart.

5. Listening helps you understand others.

6. Listening wins you respect.

7. Listening defuses anger in others.

8. Listening builds self-esteem in others.

9. Listening increases your knowledge power.

10. Listening brings you friendship and caring from others.

The Rewards Of Personal Listening

POCKET PACKET FORMAT

— COMMUNICATION —

Activity Five

Write an original skit or role play that portrays one or more of the following barriers to good listening. Make it both entertaining and informative if you can!

1. Physical discomfort (too hot, tired, or sick)
2. Interruptions (from noise or distractions in physical environment)
3. Mental preoccupations (from other things on your mind)
4. Predetermined answers (pat or flippant reactions or responses)
5. Boredom (lack of interest in other person or message)
6. Preoccupied with own self (self-absorbed)
7. Selective listening (hearing only part of what is being said)
8. Dislike for other person (prejudiced feelings and opinions)

Activity Six

Body language can influence one's ability to listen or be heard. Design a comic strip about a listening situation and use one or more of these nonverbal behaviors as part of your storyline.

1. Raising an eyebrow
2. Nodding your head
3. Frowning or scowling
4. Rolling your eyes
5. Hanging your head
6. Squinting or narrowing your eyes
7. Folding your arms across your chest
8. Slumping in your chair
9. Shrugging your shoulders
10. Having direct eye contact
11. Looking delighted or eager
12. Changing your posture
13. Crossing your legs
14. Tilting your head down
15. Tapping your fingers or your toes

The Rewards Of Personal Listening

POCKET PACKET FORMAT

── COMMUNICATION ──

Activity Seven

Choose a peer and express your thoughts, feelings, experiences, and ideas on each of the following topics. Take turns serving as listener and speaker. When you are listening, do not interrupt, ask questions, or give advice. Instead, listen with understanding, with eye contact, with positive body language, and with an open, relaxed posture. When the instructions tell you to do a listening check, summarize what the talker said by paraphrasing, in your own words, what your partner said.

TOPIC ONE: Who is your favorite book character and what makes him or her so special to you? How are you like or different from this character?

LISTENING CHECK: Summarize what the speaker said about his or her favorite book character.

TOPIC TWO: If you could write a best-selling novel for kids, what would it be about?

LISTENING CHECK: As I understand it, you . . .

TOPIC THREE: In all of language, what are the three most beautiful words that you know and why?

LISTENING CHECK: It seems you . . .

TOPIC FOUR: If you could give advice to young children about learning to read and the importance of books, what would you say?

LISTENING CHECK: It sounds like . . .

The Rewards Of Personal Listening

POCKET PACKET FORMAT

— COMMUNICATION —

Activity Eight

Choose one or more of these creative listening activities to complete.

1. Make a list of your favorite sounds from nature.

2. Write down five things you love to have other people say about or to you.

3. Brainstorm a list of sounds that you associate with each of these colors: red, green, blue, orange, purple, yellow, and black.

4. Design a simple listening exercise for others to follow. It might involve the use of numbers, directions, or rhyming patterns.

5. Choose a short story to read to the class. Design a series of simple drawings or pictures to represent important people, places, events, or things in the story. Mix up the set of drawings and have others place them in the correct sequence as you read the story.

6. Prepare a tape recording of familiar sounds around the home, school, or community. Play these back for your peers and see how many of them can guess the source of each sound. Consider such sounds as a running faucet, a ringing doorbell, or a chirping bird.

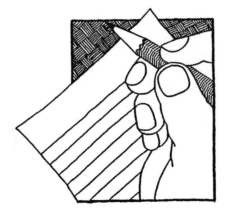

Creative Dramas That Teach

POCKET PACKET FORMAT

— COMMUNICATION —

Activity One

Think of a simple incident that has very distinct images and potential movements associated with it. For example, a bunch of balloons floating in the air at a circus, a cup of kernels exploding in a popcorn machine, a school of fish swimming in the water of a mountain stream, or a large puddle of glue spilled on the classroom floor. Write an action paragraph describing details of what is happening using colorful language and words that express movement. Read this paragraph aloud and have a group of friends try to "act out" what is happening.

Activity Two

Try acting out one of the following situations without saying any words or giving yourself away. You are to pantomime actions and behaviors most commonly associated with the situation itself. Have others try to guess what you are portraying.

1. You are a special type of toy in a store window.

2. You are eating a particular type of food that is difficult to manage.

3. You are working at a unique job or occupation.

4. You are visiting a tourist attraction in an unfamiliar community.

5. You are a mechanical object.

Creative Dramas That Teach

POCKET PACKET FORMAT

— COMMUNICATION —

Activity Three

In this activity, you are to react to all the different sights, sounds, tastes, and textures that are associated with a particular setting. Choose one or more of the ideas listed here and practice "taking in your surroundings through your five senses." What do you see, hear, touch, or smell? How does it affect you?

1. A visit to an airport
2. A trip to the supermarket
3. A ride on a crowded bus
4. A bystander at a parade
5. A walk at the beach

Activity Four

We often vary the speed, pitch, projection, and inflection of our voices in a speech or conversation depending upon the circumstances of the situation. Work with a friend and practice speaking to one another in the situations given below. Can you add others to the list?

1. A person on shore giving directions to the driver of a boat trying to dock his or her oversized craft in a storm.
2. Two people trying to carry on a conversation at a pep rally.
3. Two hearing impaired friends at a senior citizen dinner who are trying to reminisce about "old times."
4. Two firemen giving directions to one another while one is on the roof of a burning two story building and the other is on the ground holding a water hose.

Creative Dramas That Teach

Activity Five

Get a book of short plays or skits from the school media center. Work with a group of friends to read these aloud without having a chance to practice or rehearse first. What are the results? Next, read through the scripts once or twice before performing them in front of others. How does this make a difference? Finally, work with a small group to write and produce a short commercial on an imaginary product. Write this in a short play or skit format. Perform these for one another using all the "drama" you can muster!

Activity Six

Choose a picture book from the school media center that has a strong emotional appeal for the reader. Practice reading this book aloud for expression and impact. Then try telling the story from memory. In your opinion, which version is better and why? Do you think there is an "art" to storytelling?

Sit with a group of friends in a large circle. Your task is to make up a story, making certain that each person in the circle has time to contribute his or her ideas to the story. Each person should have equal time in telling his or her piece of the story and should be certain to pick up the storyline where the previous storyteller left off. The last person in the circle should conclude the story in some meaningful way. You may want to tape your group story for posterity!

Creative Dramas That Teach

POCKET PACKET FORMAT

— COMMUNICATION —

Activity Seven

You are to pretend that you have been invited to give a keynote speech to a group of distinguished guests who recognize you as a national expert on a subject of your choice. You are to start your speech with the words:

"Thank you for inviting me here today as an expert on the

subject of _____ ."

You are to pick a sophisticated topic such as heart transplants, exotic birds, the effects of rigor mortis, oceanography, etc. Give your speech as though you are indeed an authority on the subject, providing explicit details and descriptions of your work, experiences, and observations. Make up your facts and sources of information as if you were a "walking encyclopedia!"

Activity Eight

Work with a friend to discuss a controversial issue that is interesting to both of you, but is also an issue about which each of you feels somewhat differently. Carry on a conversation with one another for three minutes during which each of you expresses his or her opinion in an ongoing dialogue.

Halfway through the conversation, switch positions and begin expressing the other person's point of view.

What Tickles Your Funny Bone?

POCKET PACKET FORMAT

─ SCHOOL CULTURE AND ACADEMIC SURVIVAL ─

Activity One

Rate your sense of humor on a scale of 1 to 5 for each of the following statements. Consider that a "1" is very characteristic of you while a "5" is very uncharacteristic of you.

1. My teacher considers my sense of humor to be an asset in the classroom.
2. My family values my sense of humor at home.
3. I can laugh at my own mistakes and when others poke fun at me.
4. I laugh alone when I think something is funny.
5. I enjoy cartoons, comedy shows, jokes, and other humorous sources.
6. My sense of humor helps me during difficult times or times of stress.
7. My sense of humor makes it hard for friends and family to stay mad at me.
8. I sometimes act silly for no reason at all.
9. I prefer to send humorous notes, cards, or letters than more serious ones.
10. I use humor to help me learn.

What Tickles Your Funny Bone?

POCKET PACKET FORMAT

— SCHOOL CULTURE AND ACADEMIC SURVIVAL —

Activity Two

Ransack your memory to write down the historical sources of your "humor data base." List your funniest . . .

- Movie
- Television Show
- Book
- Cartoon Character
- Friend

- Family Member
- Joke
- Personal Blooper
- Incident At School
- Dream

Activity Three

Do you agree or disagree with each of the following humor-related statements? Be ready to give specific reasons and examples to support your position.

Quote One:
"People show their character in nothing more clearly than by what they think laughable." (Goethe)

Quote Two:
"Of all days, the day in which one has not laughed is surely the most wasted." (Nicholas Chamfort)

Quote Three:
"A very wise old teacher once said: 'I consider a day's teaching is wasted if we do not all have one hearty laugh.' He meant that when people laugh together, they cease to be young and old, master and pupil, worker and driver, jailer and prisoner; they become a single group of human beings enjoying its existence." (Gilbert Highet)

What Tickles Your Funny Bone?

POCKET PACKET FORMAT

─ SCHOOL CULTURE AND ACADEMIC SURVIVAL ─

Activity Four

Decide how you would go about measuring your smile and the smile of others in your class. Once you have determined this smile measurement system, conduct a series of "smile measures" to find out such facts as:

1. Who has the shortest smile? the longest smile?
2. Who has smiles of the same length?
3. Who has a smile that varies from time to time?
4. Who can use their smile to measure other objects in the room?

Activity Five

Which of the following ideas makes the most "humor sense" to you and why?

1. Humor takes work.
2. Humor involves risk-taking.
3. Humor promotes creativity and creativity promotes humor.
4. You are your own best source of humor.
5. There is a fine line between humor and tragedy.

Activity Six

Use a thesaurus to list all of the words you can find that mean the same as the word "humor." Select a few of them to write in a sentence and illustrate the ideas presented.

What Tickles Your Funny Bone?

POCKET PACKET FORMAT

─ SCHOOL CULTURE AND ACADEMIC SURVIVAL ─

Activity Seven

Create a mini-poster, flyer, or greeting card promoting these ideas:

1. The average 4-year-old laughs 400 times a day, but the average adult laughs only 15 or 16 times a day.
2. Laughing 100 times a day is the cardiovascular equivalent of 10 minutes of rowing.
3. Laughter exercises muscles in the face, arms, legs, stomach, diaphragm, thorax, and the circulatory and endocrine systems.
4. It takes only 16 facial muscles to create a smile; it takes 28 muscles to frown.

Activity Eight

Select a funny comic book, read it, and use it to complete these activities:

List the physical and personality traits of the comic book's major character. *(Knowledge)*

Summarize the plot of the comic book in your own words. *(Comprehension)*

Determine how much it would cost to purchase your comic book for every person in the class if the store manager gave you a five percent discount for quantity buying. *(Application)*

Make a list of funny comic book characters and decide which of these individuals is most like you and why. *(Analysis)*

Create a new comic book superhero or superheroine. Design the costume, symbol, and setting for your creation. *(Synthesis)*

Critique your comic book according to the following criteria: character development, story line, illustrations, color, action, length, and interest. *(Evaluation)*

What Tickles Your Funny Bone?

POCKET PACKET FORMAT

— SCHOOL CULTURE AND ACADEMIC SURVIVAL —

Activity Nine

Design a "book of humor" that contains examples of your favorite and funniest entries. Visit the media center to locate all different types of humorous resources and use these to locate an entry in each of the following categories:

- Your favorite "knock knock" joke
- Your favorite riddle
- Your favorite pun
- Your favorite tongue twister
- Your favorite "stink pink"
- Your favorite limerick
- Your favorite daffy definition
- Your favorite one liner
- Your favorite silly verse
- Your favorite wacky insult

Copy these down and illustrate them. Create a cover, title page, dedication page, and "giggliography" for your humor book.

Activity Ten

To make your humor work for you, try doing one or more of the following tasks:

- Maintain a Laughter Log (Humor Diary).
- Start a Humor File (Index File).
- Create a Humor Album (Photograph or Picture Scrapbook).

Mathematical Connections

POCKET PACKET FORMAT

┌─ SCHOOL CULTURE AND ACADEMIC SURVIVAL ─┐

Activity One

Go on a walking or driving tour of your neighborhood and community to discover the connections between geometry and architecture. Notice what shapes and angles are used in the construction of houses, buildings, and recreational facilities. Take photos of and notes on what you see, or browse through magazines and cut out pictures that are replicas of or variations on what you see. Next, decide on a special location—such as a desert, rain forest, mountain top, urban city, or coastal area—to design the house of your dreams. Make your house creative by using unusual combinations of geometric shapes and angles.

Activity Two

Study the math tic tac toe gameboard to the right and note that the three pictures have something in common with one another. What is it? Can you complete the other six squares with math terms or concepts in a similar fashion for others to figure out?

	TIMES STOCKS INCREASE TEN BUCKS A SHARE	
	$10.00 shirt	
	DIMES $5.00 / DIMES	

Mathematical Connections

POCKET PACKET FORMAT

— SCHOOL CULTURE AND ACADEMIC SURVIVAL —

Activity Three

Sometimes schools pass a number of rules that don't make much sense to the students they are designed to serve. Many of these rules are carried over from year to year and are not reviewed or updated on a regular basis. Work with a group of peers to complete each of the following "starter statements" about the rules in your school, especially as they apply to your math class.

1. There should be a rule against kids in math who . . .
2. There should be a rule against math textbooks that . . .
3. There should be a rule against math teachers who . . .
4. There should be a rule against parents or guardians who say that math is . . .
5. There should be a rule against politicians who want math students to . . .
6. There should be rewards in math for . . .
7. If I could write one rule for my math class, this is what it would say . . .

Activity Four

Overlapping circles in math are called Venn diagrams. They are used to show similarities and differences between two or more people, places, or things. The part where the circles overlap is called the intersection of the circles, and it represents what the people, places, or things have in common with one another. You are to draw a pair of intersecting circles to represent you and your best friend. Write down the things that make you different in the non-intersecting parts of the circle and the ways you are alike in the intersection of the circle. Consider physical, personality, and social traits as well as individual preferences, statistics, and interests. Next, draw a third intersecting circle and let it represent a mutual friend that you both have. Show the common traits all three of you share in the intersection this time. Can you add a fourth or fifth friend to this diagram and make it work?

Mathematical Connections

POCKET PACKET FORMAT

─ SCHOOL CULTURE AND ACADEMIC SURVIVAL ─

Activity Five

Divide your class into six small groups and provide each group with a bag of assorted gumdrops (in size and color), a box of toothpicks, and a different task card based on the activities outlined below. Set a time limit and have each group complete the activities as directed. Allow time for sharing the results.

GROUP NUMBER ONE:

Knowledge Task: List as many wobbly things as you can think of.

Comprehension Task: Summarize the job qualifications and key responsibilities of a "rainbowologist."

Application Task: Construct a bird with the toothpicks and gumdrops.

Analysis Task: Compare and contrast pleasures of the mind with pleasures of the emotions.

Synthesis Task: Create an original limerick.

Evaluation Task: Decide on the most important invention that changed history. List your criteria.

GROUP NUMBER TWO:

Knowledge Task: List as many squeaky things as you can think of.

Comprehension Task: Summarize the job qualifications and key responsibilities of a "chocolatologist."

Application Task: Construct a wild animal using the toothpicks and gumdrops.

Analysis Task: Compare and contrast the pleasures of music with the pleasures of art.

Synthesis Task: Create an original joke involving numbers.

Evaluation Task: Decide on the most important discovery of the 20th century. List your criteria.

GROUP NUMBER THREE:

Knowledge Task: List as many spongy things as you can think of.

Comprehension Task: Summarize the job qualifications and key responsibilities of a "humorologist."

Application Task: Construct an insect using the toothpicks and gumdrops.

Analysis Task: Compare and contrast the pleasures of the workplace with pleasures of the home.

Synthesis Task: Create an original metaphor using a number.

Evaluation Task: Decide on the most important nominee for this year's Nobel prize winner for peace. List your criteria.

Mathematical Connections

POCKET PACKET FORMAT

— SCHOOL CULTURE AND ACADEMIC SURVIVAL —

Activity Five (continued)

GROUP NUMBER FOUR:

Knowledge Task: List as many infinite things as you can think of.

Comprehension Task: Summarize the job qualifications and key responsibilities of a "funtologist."

Application Task: Construct a sea creature with the toothpicks and gumdrops.

Analysis Task: Compare and contrast the pleasures of the palate with the pleasures of an aroma.

Synthesis Task: Create a pun that plays with numbers.

Evaluation Task: Decide on the most important societal trend for the 1990s. List your criteria.

GROUP NUMBER FIVE:

Knowledge Task: List as many glittery things as you can think of.

Comprehension Task: Summarize the job qualifications and key responsibilities of a "musicologist."

Application Task: Construct a reptile from the toothpicks and gumdrops.

Analysis Task: Compare and contrast the pleasures of reading with the pleasures of writing.

Synthesis Task: Create an original riddle about numbers.

Evaluation Task: Decide on the most important innovation/change in the history of education. List your criteria.

GROUP NUMBER SIX:

Knowledge Task: List as many stretchable things as you can think of.

Comprehension Task: Summarize the job qualifications and key responsibilities of a "geometrologist."

Application Task: Construct an amphibian with the toothpicks and gumdrops.

Analysis Task: Compare and contrast the pleasures of solitude with the pleasures of relationships.

Synthesis Task: Create an original nursery rhyme that includes a number.

Evaluation Task: Decide on the most important influence on today's early adolescent. List your criteria.

Mathematical Connections

POCKET PACKET FORMAT

⎯ SCHOOL CULTURE AND ACADEMIC SURVIVAL ⎯

Activity Six

Use assorted reference tools to uncover the set of facts that will help you to solve these math problems.

ENGLISH: What is the combined total if you were to add the birth years of these five popular authors of novels for kids: Esther Forbes *(Johnny Tremain)*, Laura Ingalls Wilder *(The Little House books)*, Elizabeth George Speare *(The Witch of Blackbird Pond)*, Carol Ryrie Brink *(Caddie Woodlawn)*, and Christopher Collier *(My Brother Sam Is Dead)*.

MUSIC: What percentage of the instruments in a world-class orchestra is most likely to be strings and what percentage is most likely to be brass?

GEOGRAPHY: In square miles, how much bigger is Lake Superior than Lake Huron in the United States?

SCIENCE: If you multiplied the diameter of the planet Mercury with the diameter of the planet Mars, what would their product be?

SOCIAL STUDIES: Add the total number of Representatives and the total number of Senators in the United States Congress and divide by five.

NOW . . . try making up some research math problems of your own for others to figure out.

Activity Seven

Cover a bulletin board with a large piece of white paper. Across the top of the paper, write out the words "World's Largest Math Worksheet." Have the class develop a number code for the alphabet and then write out their own names using the code as a logo. Construct a "code logo key" to place in one corner of the large mural. During the week, encourage students to make up a series of math and word problems from lessons they are working on and to write them out on the mural, making certain to sign their names in code to each problem they contribute. As time permits, students should also try to solve any of the problems, making certain to sign their work in code for identification purposes. At the end of the week, tally the problems and solutions to determine who the math whiz kids are for the class.

Mathematical Connections

POCKET PACKET FORMAT

— SCHOOL CULTURE AND ACADEMIC SURVIVAL —

Activity Eight

Complete the following math tasks at home. Record your results and share with others in your class.

1. Find 10 different things in your house that weigh between five and ten pounds.

2. Predict the most common color of food located on the most crowded shelf in your kitchen cupboard. Test your prediction.

3. Determine the average age of persons living in your house.

4. Use a paper plate to construct a pie chart on how you spend a typical 24-hour day during the week and another one for how you spend a typical 24-hour day on a weekend.

5. Measure the area of each major living space in your home or apartment. Arrange these in order from smallest to largest.

6. Use a deck of playing cards to invent a new game that involves math. Write out the rules for your game and teach others to play it.

7. Search your house for things that are an exact square.

8. Organize a "rummage" book and toy sale for your class and ask friends to bring in books, toys, and games from home that they don't want any longer. Price them and conduct your sale!

9. Collect all of the coins or loose change from members of your family and categorize them by dates. Graph your results.

10. List five to ten items from your bedroom that measure more than one meter.

Mathematical Connections

POCKET PACKET FORMAT

─ SCHOOL CULTURE AND ACADEMIC SURVIVAL ─

Activity Nine

Organize a theme day related to the world of math in some way. Try to schedule one day a month for this purpose. Some themes to consider might be:

1. **Backwards Day (Negative Numbers):** On this day kids can wear an article of clothing inside-out or backwards. They can sit on their chairs backwards and they can do their math worksheets in reverse order. Try doing the daily schedule backwards, and try giving them answers to problems and having them come up with the questions, Jeopardy-style.

2. **Symmetry Day:** On this day, kids can create and wear to class tee shirts or hats that are symmetrical in design. They can study symmetry, make symmetrical drawings, and go on a playground walk looking for symmetry in nature. The second half of the math class schedule can be a duplicate of the first half of the schedule in the way it is conducted and the way material is presented.

3. **Measurement Day:** On this day kids can spend their math time measuring everything in sight. They can also measure their own height using several different units ranging from nonstandard to standard units of measure. They can engage in simple timed math tasks and can prepare snacks that require measurement in their preparation.

Activity Ten

In this activity, each student in the class creates an original word problem in math and figures out the answer. The student then takes two pieces of blank paper and writes out the problem on one sheet and the solution on the other sheet. Collect the word problems and their solutions. Mix them up and give one word problem or a solution to each student and have each pin it on his or her chest. Each student then attempts to locate the person in the room whose solution matches the word problem on his or her chest and vice versa.

Math And The Imagination

FILE FOLDER FORMAT

─ SCHOOL CULTURE AND ACADEMIC SURVIVAL ─

Activity One

On a clean piece of paper, make a random set of dots all over the page. Then connect these dots in any way you choose, numbering them as you go. Examine your "follow-the-dot" shapes or pictures and describe what special images, figures, or themes you can see.

Activity Two

How do you think your life would be very different from the way it is today if . . .

- . . . you became 100 years old?
- . . . you won the lottery for $1,000,000?
- . . . you gained 50 pounds?
- . . . your I.Q. was raised by 50 points?
- . . . you were expelled from school for 60 days?
- . . . you were 8 feet tall and still growing?
- . . . you moved 10 times in 10 years?
- . . . you could eat only 1000 calories a day?

Math And The Imagination

FILE FOLDER FORMAT

— SCHOOL CULTURE AND ACADEMIC SURVIVAL —

Activity Three

Draw a game board that has five rows down with eight different geometric shapes across. Each row across should have at least four different shapes, but these may be repeated more than once in each row. No two rows, down or across, should have the same pattern of shape placements. Invent a game to go with your new game board. What are the rules? How does one move? How does one win or lose?

Activity Four

Study the word problems below. To solve these problems, count the letters that make up the words in each line. This will give you the numbers to work with.

Addition:
```
    ( 4)  pigs
    ( 5)  goats
    ( 6)  horses
    ( 7)  kittens
    ( 8)  roosters
+   ( 9)  barnyards
    (39)  typical and terrific farm
          scene in the country
```

Subtraction:
```
    (10)  four o'clock
–   ( 8)  homework
    ( 2)  TV
```

Multiplication:
```
    ( 6)  scoops
x   ( 5)  cones
    (30)  super-fantastic
          multi-level treats
```

Division:
```
                ( 5)  panic
( 5) lions / (25)  opened, unlocked
                   circus cages
```

Make up a set of word problems that tell about you. Be sure to include a variety of problems to show off your various math skills.

Math And The Imagination

— SCHOOL CULTURE AND ACADEMIC SURVIVAL —

Activity Five

On a large sheet of paper, draw a make-believe creature that has at least nine of the following features:

antenna	eye	horn	snout	mouth	leg	hair	wing
whisker	finger	fin	tail	nose	foot	ear	tusk

Assign a number value to each body part (for instance, 7 for a finger, 13 for a fin). Then, design and compute a set of number sentence problems that make use of your creature for the answers.

Examples: 5 times a fin equals 65. (5 X 13 = 65)
100 minus 2 fingers equals 86. (100 - 14 = 86)

Write your problems on the front of your creature, and put your answers on the back. Ask a classmate to work your "Creature Feature" sentence problems.

Activity Six

Choose one of the following writing tasks:

(1) Write a love story between a circle and a square.

(2) Write an autobiography of a compass or a protractor.

(3) Write a number rebus story.

(4) Write a poem of couplets using the numbers one through ten.

(5) Write a paragraph that has the name of a number hidden in it.

(6) Write a fable to tell why Friday the 13th is an unlucky day.

(7) Write a play about the Baker's Dozen.

(8) Write a series of number jokes or riddles.

(9) Write a secret message using a number code.

(10) Write a series of word problems using personal numbers that have meaning to you and your friends.

Math And The Imagination

FILE FOLDER FORMAT

—SCHOOL CULTURE AND ACADEMIC SURVIVAL—

Activity Seven

Ask students to think of an unusual, unique place to create and advertise a place for math lovers. They might want to invent Metric Village, Math City, Geometry Junction, Symmetry Square, or Computer Community. Each student should then design a travel folder of five sections to answer the following questions:

- What is it? (name and description)
- Where is it? (location with map and legend)
- When is it open? (chart of times and events)
- Why is it special? (series of drawings or diagrams)
- How did it come to be? (outline of its history or beginnings)

Activity Eight

Did you know that you can use fractions to make up a series of word puzzles? Study the examples below and then make up a few of your own.

What is the first ⅖ of "class?" Answer: cl

What is the last ³⁄₁₀ of "friendship?" Answer: hip

What is the middle ¼ of "food?" Answer: oo

How's Your IQ
(Innovation Quotient)?

FILE FOLDER FORMAT

── SELF-CONCEPT AND RELATIONSHIPS ──

Activity One

You are to invent a country located anywhere in the world. Use the outline below to help you introduce this new country to others who want to learn more about it. Design a travel folder to convey this information.

1. What is its name?

2. Where is its exact location?

3. What type of people inhabit the country? What unique physical and character traits do they have?

4. Describe the climate and terrain.

5. What products and services does it produce to maintain its economy?

6. What type of government does it have?

7. Describe the historical sites and tourist attractons of the area.

How's Your IQ
(Innovation Quotient)?

— SELF-CONCEPT AND RELATIONSHIPS —

Activity Two

Select a culture of special interest to you and create a culture box based on that culture. Locate, make, or draw pictures of a wide variety of artifacts that represent that culture and place them in the box. For each artifact, complete an "information tag" that tells what the artifact represents and why it is important.

Activity Three

Decide on a social studies topic and develop a "hands-on" museum exhibit that tells something about it. Try to make your exhibit appeal to all five senses by including something to see, touch, hear, smell, and taste. Can your exhibit contain something for viewers to do?

How's Your IQ
(Innovation Quotient)?

FILE FOLDER FORMAT

SELF-CONCEPT AND RELATIONSHIPS

Activity Four

Plan a business enterprise where you become an entrepreneur and provide either a service or product to interested customers. Decide what you will name your business, where it will be located, the hours you will keep, and the advertising you will do. Some unusual business ideas to consider might be:

- Balloon Bouquet Designer
- Party Planner
- Button Maker
- Homework Helper
- Newsletter Publisher
- Photographer
- Snack Vendor
- Rock Painter
- T-shirt Painter
- Puppet Maker

How's Your IQ
(Innovation Quotient)?

FILE FOLDER FORMAT

── SELF-CONCEPT AND RELATIONSHIPS ──

Activity Five

Compile a poetry anthology based on a social theme or subject of your choice.

Choose a theme such as cultures, landmarks, food, famous battles, unusual places, heroes, or nature. Browse through a large number of poetry books and select poems based on that theme. Copy each poem on a piece of drawing paper and illustrate it. Prepare a booklet of your poems complete with cover, table of contents, dedication page, and bibliography.

How's Your IQ
(Innovation Quotient)?

FILE FOLDER FORMAT

— SELF-CONCEPT AND RELATIONSHIPS —

Activity Six

Write a puppet show, construct your puppets, and put on a performance. Will you make stick puppets, finger puppets, paper bag puppets, sock puppets, or paper plate puppets? Try to create a puppet show that represents some period or group in history. Consider a script about pioneers, cowboys, pilgrims, slaves, or space explorers.

Activity Seven

Plan an International Fair for your classroom or school. Work with a group of students to organize an International Fair that has display booths, food booths, information booths, game booths, retail booths, and "make-and-take" booths. You might also want to organize demonstration sessions that include dance, story-telling, skits, and craft making.

Investigating A Road Map

INVESTIGATION CARD FORMAT

SELF-CONCEPT AND RELATIONSHIPS

HOW TO USE . . .

Using a road map, the student may choose to:

- complete only the cards which correlate to a particular level of Bloom's Taxonomy,

  or . . .

- select only the cards in which he or she is interested,

  or . . .

- (if he or she is particularly ambitious and needs a real challenge) complete all eighteen of the ROAD MAP Investigation Cards.

Listed below are Bloom's Taxonomy levels and the corresponding task card numbers for each.

KNOWLEDGE 1, 2, 3

COMPREHENSION 4, 5, 6

APPLICATION 7, 8, 9

ANALYSIS 10, 11, 12

SYNTHESIS 13, 14, 15

EVALUATION 16, 17, 18

1

Define "cartography."
Write the definition
in a complete sentence.

2

List the many different
types of information
one is likely to find
on a typical road map
for any of the fifty United States.

Investigating A Road Map

INVESTIGATION CARD FORMAT

SELF-CONCEPT AND RELATIONSHIPS

3

Select a letter of the alphabet and write down at least 25 cities or towns that begin with that letter. Use a road map of your state for this purpose. Put each city or town on a separate slip of paper, mix up the papers, and rearrange them again in alphabetical order.

4

Explain the purpose of the legend on your road map.

5

In your own words, tell what the index of a map is used for and how this relates to the index of a reference book.

6

Summarize how one can use the mileage chart on your road map.

Investigating A Road Map

INVESTIGATION CARD FORMAT

— SELF-CONCEPT AND RELATIONSHIPS —

7

Close your eyes and point to two different places on your map that are some distance apart.
Use the mileage chart to determine the total distance between these two points, using at least three different routes to get from one place to the other.

8

Use the legend on your map to help locate at least one specific site for each category listed below. Record your responses.

- a divided highway
- an interstate highway
- a roadside park or rest area
- a recreation area
- an airport
- a railroad
- the state capital
- a city of 25,000 to 50,000 people
- a historic site

9

Plan a seven day sight-seeing field trip of your state to take with your class using a tour bus. Where will you go, sleep, and eat? What will you see and do? How much will it cost each student for food, lodging, fees, and souvenirs?

10

Compare and contrast any two parts of the state represented on your road map. Consider location, population, landmarks, history, and standard of living.

Investigating A Road Map

INVESTIGATION CARD FORMAT

— SELF-CONCEPT AND RELATIONSHIPS —

11

Using the map and doing some research, choose the part of your state that would be the most desirable in which to live and work.

12

Determine the most unique features of your state by analyzing the map and using it as your primary data source.

13

Create a "visitor's packet" for your state that would be available through the state's Chamber of Commerce. What kinds of things would you put in it to promote your state as an interesting place to visit?

14

What do you think your road map would say to a billboard, a blueprint, and a compass? Draw balloons and figures to show the conversations that might take place among them.

Investigating A Road Map

INVESTIGATION CARD FORMAT

SELF-CONCEPT AND RELATIONSHIPS

15

Use the information on your road map to create a puzzle, activity, and coloring book that could be sold as a learning tool to kids in your community.

16

Rate your state on a scale of 1 to 5 in each of the following areas, with 1 being excellent and 5 being poor:

- climate
- geography
- history
- business & industry options
- natural resources
- education

Be sure you can defend each of your ratings.

17

Give five reasons why your state should or should not be given this year's Golden State Award. What criteria will you use for this purpose?

18

Decide on a new flower, animal, and slogan for your state. Validate your choices with research and evidence to support your position.

Investigating A Baseball Card Collection

INVESTIGATION CARD FORMAT

── SELF-CONCEPT AND RELATIONSHIPS ──

HOW TO USE . . .

Using a baseball card collection, the student may choose to:

- complete only the cards which correlate to a particular level of Bloom's Taxonomy,

    or . . .

- select only the cards in which he or she is interested,

    or . . .

- (if he or she is particularly ambitious and needs a real challenge) complete all eighteen of the BASEBALL CARDS Investigation Cards.

Listed below are Bloom's Taxonomy levels and the corresponding task card numbers for each.

KNOWLEDGE 1, 2, 3

COMPREHENSION 4, 5, 6

APPLICATION 7, 8, 9

ANALYSIS 10, 11, 12

SYNTHESIS 13, 14, 15

EVALUATION 16, 17, 18

1

List as many reasons as you can for the popularity of trading cards—especially baseball cards—among kids today.

2

Write down the types of information contained on baseball trading cards.

Investigating A Baseball Card Collection

INVESTIGATION CARD FORMAT

SELF-CONCEPT AND RELATIONSHIPS

3

Record the names of the players in your collection of baseball cards in alphabetical order using their last names only.

4

In your own words, explain what "lessons in life" can be learned from the players in your baseball collection.

5

Describe the dimensions and layout of the typical baseball playing field and grounds that are used by the American and National League players in your baseball collection.

6

Summarize reasons that the players in your baseball collection would consider baseball America's favorite sport or pastime.

Investigating A Baseball Card Collection

INVESTIGATION CARD FORMAT

SELF-CONCEPT AND RELATIONSHIPS

7

Conduct a survey in your class to determine which baseball player, team, or position represented in your collection of baseball cards is the favorite of students in the classroom. Graph your results.

8

Select a baseball card from your collection and use it to construct a series of word problems.
Solve the problems and record the answers.

9

Use your baseball card collection to demonstrate application of math skills that involve comparing, averaging, and ordering (tallest to shortest, heaviest to lightest, best to poorest batting average).

10

Study the players in your baseball collection and decide which five skills are most important for a player to have in order to be considered a candidate for the Baseball Hall of Fame.

Investigating A Baseball Card Collection

INVESTIGATION CARD FORMAT

SELF-CONCEPT AND RELATIONSHIPS

11

Compare and contrast any two players in your card collection who play the same position but on different teams. What conclusions can you draw?

12

Read the poem "Casey At Bat" by Lawrence Thayer. Determine which player in your card collection would most closely resemble Casey in skill, personality, or appearance.

13

Create a travel game for kids or an indoor learning game for kids based on the theme of baseball and using the cards in your baseball collection as a springboard for the game. Give your game a name, rules, and set of procedures for playing.

14

Invent a new major league baseball team of the future. Include information and rationale about each of the following decisions:
- City in which it is located
- Name, logo, mascot, and colors of team
- Uniform design for the players
- Salary range of the players
- Background and personality of the coach
- Design of the baseball stadium and playing field
- Design of the ticket and plans for ticket sales

Pick one player from your baseball card collection to play on this team and give reasons for your choice.

Investigating A
Baseball Card Collection

INVESTIGATION CARD FORMAT

SELF-CONCEPT AND RELATIONSHIPS

15

Plan a baseball "theme day" for your class. Encourage students to come dressed as their favorite player in the trading card collection. Plan a series of baseball-related events, serve baseball-type food, conduct baseball photo sessions, and read baseball books and magazines.

16

Have each student in the class prepare a one-page biographical sketch of a favorite player in his or her baseball collection. Establish a Classroom Baseball Hall of Fame with criteria for selection of candidates. Hold an election to choose five baseball players to receive this honor. Be able to give reasons for each choice.

17

Defend or negate this statement: "Female players should be eligible to play professional baseball."

18

Rank order the difficulty and importance of all the playing positions in baseball. Establish a range of salaries based on your rank order and be able to document your decisions.

Investigating Rubik's Cube

INVESTIGATION CARD FORMAT

— PROBLEM-SOLVING AND DECISION-MAKING —

HOW TO USE . . .

Using a Rubik's Cube, the student may choose to:

- complete only the cards which correlate to a particular level of Bloom's Taxonomy,

  or . . .

- select only the cards in which he or she is interested,

  or . . .

- (if he or she is particularly ambitious and needs a real challenge) complete all eighteen of the RUBIK'S CUBE Investigation Cards.

Listed below are Bloom's Taxonomy levels and the corresponding task card numbers for each.

KNOWLEDGE 1, 2, 3

COMPREHENSION 4, 5, 6

APPLICATION 7, 8, 9

ANALYSIS 10, 11, 12

SYNTHESIS 13, 14, 15

EVALUATION 16, 17, 18

1

Count the number of cubes that make up a Rubik's Cube.

2

Tabulate the number of faces that can be seen on the small individual cubes that make up the Rubik's Cube.

Investigating Rubik's Cube

INVESTIGATION CARD FORMAT

— PROBLEM-SOLVING AND DECISION-MAKING —

3

Identify the colors of the faces on the Rubik's Cube.

4

Compare a Rubik's Cube to a die. How are they alike? How are they different?

5

Discuss the procedure for working the Rubik's Cube.

6

Explain the object of the game.

Investigating Rubik's Cube

INVESTIGATION CARD FORMAT

┌─ PROBLEM-SOLVING AND DECISION-MAKING ─┐

7

Determine the volume
of the Rubik's Cube.

8

Compute the area
of one side of
the Rubik's Cube.

9

Demonstrate and discuss
how the Rubik's Cube works.

10

Survey your classmates
to determine:

- how many have worked a
  Rubik's Cube,
- how many have solved a
  Rubik's Cube, and
- the best solution time.

Investigating Rubik's Cube

INVESTIGATION CARD FORMAT

— PROBLEM-SOLVING AND DECISION-MAKING —

11

Examine the various
moving parts.
What other shapes
can be created?

12

Make inferences about
what kinds of people enjoy
working a Rubik's Cube
and why.

13

Devise at least
five new uses
for the Rubik's Cube.

14

Design a step-by-step
manual for using and
solving the Rubik's
Cube. Illustrate it.

Investigating Rubik's Cube

INVESTIGATION CARD FORMAT

— PROBLEM-SOLVING AND DECISION-MAKING —

15

Create a Rubik's Cube
with a whole new look.

16

Assess the value of
spending your time working
a Rubik's Cube. Explain.

17

Compare the merits
of a Rubik's Cube to
another hand-held
manipulative game.

18

Conclude what effect, if
any, games such as the
Rubik's Cube have on
developing one's ability
to solve problems.

Be A Junior Economist

FILE FOLDER FORMAT

— PROBLEM-SOLVING AND DECISION-MAKING —

Activity One

An ECONOMIST is the name given to an expert on the buying and selling of goods and services. This person understands the meaning of many special economic ideas. Economists help us to control the magic world of spending, earning, saving, and producing.

Make a colorful set of flash cards for each of the following economic words. On one side of the card put the word. On the other side of the card put the definition and the word used correctly in a sentence. Add a simple picture where possible.

> Competition, Consumer, Producer, Profit, Goods, Services, Capital, Natural Resources, Labor, Assembly Line, Economics, Market

Activity Two

A person who makes useful things or who does useful work is called a PRODUCER. A producer who makes useful things is a PRODUCER of GOODS. A producer who does useful work for others without making a product is a PRODUCER of SERVICES.

Choose any ten students in your class and write down their names and what their moms or dads or guardians do for a living. Decide whether these adults are producers of goods or producers of services. Set your work up in chart or graph form.

Activity Three

Most people have a need to work hard. All human work or effort is called LABOR and this includes a person's time, skills, and effort. There are over 22,000 different types of work or labor that people can do.

Get a large piece of paper and write out an Occupation Alphabet from A to Z. Write each letter down the side of the paper and try to come up with three jobs for each letter. Choose one job and think of many others that are related to it.

> EXAMPLE: Airline Pilot (Air Controller, Flight Attendant, Ticket Seller)

Be A
Junior Economist

FILE FOLDER FORMAT

— PROBLEM-SOLVING AND DECISION-MAKING —

Activity Four

A person who makes useful things to sell or who does useful work for others is called a PRODUCER. Choose an adult worker or producer to interview and ask him or her the questions listed below. Share this information by preparing a one-minute talk about the person you interviewed and his or her job.

1. Why did you choose your job?
2. What skills or training do you need?
3. What do you like about your job?
4. What don't you like about your job?
5. What problems do you have to solve in your job?
6. If you had it to do all over again, would you choose the same job? Why?

Activity Five

Everybody is a CONSUMER because a consumer is anyone who buys or uses goods and services. Goods are products we need or want. Services are the jobs we pay someone else to do for us. Make three mini-billboard dioramas, one that shows things you use or buy often, one that shows things you use or buy once in a while, and one that shows things you seldom use or buy. Study your finished dioramas and write a good paragraph that summarizes: types of items that appear in each diorama; diorama that has most and least expensive items; diorama that has items used up most rapidly; diorama that involves making the greatest decisions.

Activity Six

The U.S. has a MARKET ECONOMY. This means that buyers and sellers get together in various locations to buy and sell their goods and services. Most products can be sold in several different types of markets. Milk, for example, can be sold in dairies, grocery stores, schools, and restaurants. See how many different places or markets you can think of where the following items might be sold. Try to name at least five possible markets for each item: *paperback books, ice cream, footballs, records.*
(Hint: Use the Yellow Pages for ideas.)

Be A
Junior Economist

FILE FOLDER FORMAT

— PROBLEM-SOLVING AND DECISION-MAKING —

Activity Seven

COMPETITION is a contest between businesses with each one trying to win the buyer's money. Business people compete through better prices, service, bargains, quality, advertising, variety, and packaging.

Pretend you own a store that sells toys and competes with another in the area. Make a set of large, colorful signs similar to the ones below, only more creative, lively, and competitive.

- **The Toy Shop** (Name)
- **Parker Bros. Sold Here** (Variety)
- **Buy A Toy And Get Another Half Price** (Sale)
- **Toys Guaranteed** (Quality)
- **Free Gift Wrap With $5.00 Purchase** (Service)
- **Buy A Toy For A Child** (Slogan)

Activity Eight

Because people cannot have everything they want, it is necessary to learn how to make WISE ECONOMIC CHOICES. Whenever someone makes an economic choice, that person is deciding to buy one thing over another and has good reasons for doing so.

Divide a large piece of manila paper into six sections. Using magazine or newspaper pictures, find examples for each of the following situations: WOMAN making an economic choice; MAN making an economic choice; TEENAGER making an economic choice; SMALL CHILD making an economic choice; FAMILY making an economic choice; WORKER or BUSINESSMAN making an economic choice.

Activity Nine

CAPITAL RESOURCES are those things that help people produce other goods or services. Machines, tools, land, buildings, and equipment are all examples of capital resources needed for producing an item.

Decide on an unusual product or service to provide a customer. Design a Rube Goldberg invention or cartoon to show the many capital resources needed to make it possible. Tools, machines, equipment, and workers should all play a part in your Rube Goldberg creation.

Be A Junior Economist

FILE FOLDER FORMAT

— PROBLEM-SOLVING AND DECISION-MAKING —

Activity Ten

A WISE CONSUMER always thinks about several things before buying any product. These include price, need, quality, use, ecology, and durability. On a piece of paper divided into five columns, write down five things you would like to have as a birthday gift. Then answer these questions about each item to see which gift would be the best choice.

1. Do I need it and will I use it often?
2. Is it practical or do I want it because everybody else does?
3. Do I already have something much like it?
4. Is there a better product or another item I need more?
5. Can I make something like it for less money?
6. Can my family afford it?
7. Does producing it use up more raw materials than Earth can afford for what I'll get out of it?
8. How do I know it is a quality product?

Activity Eleven

Humans can produce more and better goods in less time and with less work through DIVISION OF LABOR. That is, a person can learn to do a specific job so well that he or she becomes a specialist. This leads to much greater skill and efficiency in the producing of a product.
Set up an assembly line to produce a product by following the steps listed below.

1. Choose a simple item to make from a craft or hobby book.
2. List the various steps or jobs necessary to make the item.
3. Find someone to do each job or step and have him or her practice.
4. Gather materials for making several of the items.
5. Organize your group into a working assembly line so that each person is doing one specific job to make the item. Time yourselves and see how many items you can mass produce in a given time period.

Be A
Junior Economist

— PROBLEM-SOLVING AND DECISION-MAKING —

Activity Twelve

Three basic types of RESOURCES are needed to produce a product. These include: RAW MATERIALS, or natural materials that come from plants, the ground, or animals; CAPITAL RESOURCES, or things needed to produce a product, such as land, tools, machines, buildings, or equipment; and HUMAN RESOURCES, or items relating to the worker, including time, knowledge, skill, and experience of those actually making the product. Design a simple diagram or flow chart to show how some product is made from scratch. Be sure to show all types of resources used in its production.

Activity Thirteen

Newspapers and magazines often help us to make wise economic choices when they publish PRODUCT REVIEWS. These reviews give us information and advice by describing all the good and bad things about a certain item for sale on the market. Choose a toy, game, or craft kit that you own. Write a product review about it, making sure to tell:

- size, price, and manufacturer of item
- design or overall purpose of item
- quality of materials used in item
- packaging of item
- appeal of item to the buyer
- overall opinion of item

Activity Fourteen

Nobody has everything he or she desires because of limited funds, limited raw materials, limited supply, or limited production of an item. This is the idea of UNLIMITED WANTS and LIMITED RESOURCES. Pretend you have the freedom and money to design the perfect school. Create the library, playground, gymnasium, cafeteria, and classrooms. Draw a simple floor plan or map of the area complete with labels and sizes. Then write a brief description of the details telling the subjects to be offered, the special equipment or materials to be available, and the unusual furniture or features to be included. Be able to explain why the perfect school as you have created it is not possible in real life.

What Makes A Leader?

─ PROBLEM-SOLVING AND DECISION-MAKING ─

Activity One

Work with a small group of peers to create a list of great leaders. Consider leaders who are artists, athletes, politicians, scientists, writers, pioneers, entertainers, and business entrepreneurs. Analyze your list of leaders and decide on the five most common traits all of these leaders share. Finally, write down the major achievement of each of these leaders.

Activity Two

Think about leaders in your class and school. What areas of leadership do they represent and what characteristics do they have in common? Develop a "Student Leadership Hall of Fame." Nominate candidates for this honor. Consider student leaders who are artists, athletes, politicians, scientists, writers, pioneers, entertainers, and business entrepreneurs. Stage an election to choose among candidates and design an award for the winners.

Activity Three

Determine the similarities and differences between leaders and heroes. Are they the same thing or can someone be considered a hero and not a leader or a leader and not a hero? Organize a debate in your classroom to argue for one of these positions. Research to gain evidence and examples to support whatever side you take.

What Makes A Leader?

— PROBLEM-SOLVING AND DECISION-MAKING —

Activity Four

The following quotations reflect leaders' views of themselves. Read each one and write a personal reaction or response to the idea presented.

1. "Great minds have purposes, others have wishes."
   (Washington Irving)

2. "The great tragedies of history occur not when right confronts wrong, but when two rights confront each other."
   (Henry Kissinger)

3. "I will not permit any man to narrow and degrade my soul by hating him."
   (Booker T. Washington)

4. "No person was ever honored for what he received; honor has been the reward for what he gave."
   (Calvin Coolidge)

5. "Nothing is particularly hard if you divide it into small jobs."
   (Henry Ford)

What Makes A Leader?

— PROBLEM-SOLVING AND DECISION-MAKING —

Activity Five

Many leaders have had role models in their lives. Define role model and think about people who have served as role models for you over the years: family members, teachers, friends, etc. Try selecting a famous role model that you admire (someone you can read about in magazines and newspapers or hear about on radio and television). Collect articles and information about this role model and put these in a scrapbook. Record your feelings about why you admire this person and how you might transfer some of his or her positive traits and strengths into your life.

What Makes A Leader?

PORTABLE DESK TOP FORMAT

— PROBLEM-SOLVING AND DECISION-MAKING —

Activity Six

Much can be learned by reading biographies of leaders who have made history in some way or another. Locate simple biographies of leaders in your school or community media center. Construct a series of "Four Square Reports" on each one. To do this, take a piece of paper and make it a perfect square. You can use 8" x 11" paper for a short report or newsprint for a longer report. Fold each corner of the square towards the center so that all points touch in the middle. On the outside of each flap, write one of the following phrases:

Who was this leader?

When and where did this leader spend most of his or her life/career?

Why is this person considered to be a leader?

What can I learn from this leader to help me?

Under each flap, write a comprehensive response to the question.

What Makes A Leader?

PORTABLE DESK TOP FORMAT

— PROBLEM-SOLVING AND DECISION-MAKING —

Activity Seven

Unfortunately, leadership sometimes carries a negative connotation, and people tend to view it with distaste. People are becoming more and more suspicious of community and national leaders because of what they read, see, and hear about them in the media. Below are some "points to ponder" about leadership. Organize a small group discussion to share individual responses to each of these situations:

1. What question are you afraid to ask political leaders in Washington D.C. because of the answer you might receive?

2. If you were to offer the President of the U.S. one tip on how he or she could be a better leader, what would you say?

3. If you could gaze into a crystal ball and see precisely what is happening in some leadership role of a member in your community, where would you look and what do you think you would see?

4. If you could live the life of a leader for a week just to see what it would be like, would you want to and, if so, whom would you pick and why?

5. Have you ever been humiliated by someone in a leadership role? If so, what happened and how did you feel?

6. What tricks do you think leaders use to get others to do what they want them to do or think what they want them to think?

7. Have you ever challenged someone in a leadership role whose ideas were wrong even though it made others angry with you?

8. What do you think is the biggest difference between what happens to leaders on television and what happens to them in the real world?

9. Whom do you dislike the most in a leadership role? What is the best thing about that person?

10. How would you act differently if there were a younger person who idolized you and tried to copy everything you did to improve his or her leadership abilities?

READ
AND
RELATE

The Sound Of The Telephone

COMMUNICATION

Read

All sounds are made by vibrating objects. Energy is needed to make objects vibrate. Loud sounds have more energy than soft sounds. The loudness of sounds is measured in decibels.

Relate

Compile a list of soft sounds, loud sounds, pleasant sounds, painful sounds, scary sounds, and soothing sounds.

Read

Pitch tells how high or low a sound is. Sounds may vary in pitch and loudness. Low-frequency sounds have low pitch. High-frequency sounds have high pitch.

Relate

Experiment to make sounds of different pitches with a glass bottle and water. Diagram or illustrate your findings.

The Sound Of The Telephone

COMMUNICATION

Read

The telephone was invented by Alexander Graham Bell in 1876, but Thomas A. Edison quickly improved it into a practical instrument that people could use. Today we find telephones in every size, color, and shape. It is expected that we will have picture phones in the near future as well.

Relate

Write a short essay discussing the advantages and disadvantages of having picture phones in the home, school, and community as a primary tool for communicating over distances with one another.

Read

When you speak to someone on the telephone, an electric signal goes from the mouthpiece which contains a small microphone. The sound waves from your voice make a diaphragm vibrate and these currents flow along wires to the other telephone. There it works the earpiece so that the other person hears you.

Relate

Make a string telephone and use it to communicate with a friend. You will need about 10 meters of string and two paper cups. Make a small hole in the bottom of each cup. Thread the ends of the string through the holes and knot them at both ends so they will not pull out of the cup. Have a friend hold one paper cup while you hold the other. Keep the string stretched tightly between you. Speak softly into your cup while your friend holds the other cup to his or her ear. You should be able to hear one another very clearly.

Let's Be Testy

COMMUNICATION

Read

Intelligence tests are designed to measure a student's potential learning ability or aptitude for learning. They contain a series of questions that ask students to analyze and interpret different types of data, drawings, figures, and situations.

Relate

Design a television game or quiz show for whiz kids who have a high intelligence and are considered to be child prodigies. Name it, describe it, and plan a preview of it. Write out a set of sample questions, tasks, or challenges to be met on this show.

Read

Achievement tests are designed to measure the general and accumulated knowledge and skills of students across several different subject areas. They contain a series of content-related questions that are most often true/false, multiple choice, matching, and short answer in format.

Relate

Choose a chapter from one of your textbooks. Design a good (but fair) true/false, multiple choice, matching, and short answer question on information from this chapter for others to answer.
How good are you at writing test questions of this type? Is it easy or hard to do?

Let's Be Testy

COMMUNICATION

Read

Aptitude tests are designed to predict the potential achievement and interest of students in areas not formally taught in school. These tests are often administered to students for purposes of determining future career interests.

Relate

Make a list of careers that interest you at the present time. Next, make a list of special skills, talents, experiences, and subjects that you need to have in order to qualify for a career of this type. Can you rewrite your list of skills, talents, experiences, and subjects in question form that might appear on an aptitude test?

Highlights Of Radio History

COMMUNICATION

Read

At the young age of 21, Guglielmo Marconi (with the help of his brother) transmitted radio signals across the hills behind their home in Bologna, Italy. They were able to interest the British Navy in the potential of the radio, and by 1897 Marconi had established Marconi's Wireless Telegraph Company. The radio became known as the "wireless" around the world.

Relate

Pretend you are the Admiral of the British Navy who has just met with the Marconi brothers to view the first "wireless" radio in action. Write a short speech telling your fellow officers about the potential for the military of this great invention.

Read

On Christmas Day and New Year's Eve, 1906, the first American radio program was broadcast by Reginald Aubrey Fessenden from Brant Rock, Massachusetts. Fessenden played the violin, gave a speech, quoted the Bible, and played a phonograph recording that charmed people around the world.

Relate

Recreate one of the first radio programs by Fessenden for the 1990s. Modernize the program by selecting instrumental music that is popular today, preparing a celebration speech about tomorrow, reading excerpts from popular poets or authors such as Dr. Seuss and Shel Silverstein, and playing CD recordings of favorite musical entertainers.

Highlights Of Radio History

COMMUNICATION

Read

In the 1930s and 1940s, radio was at the height of its popularity, offering the listener a variety of radio dramas, comedies, and game shows. People were glued to the radio broadcasts that featured such stars as Fibber McGee and Molly, ventriloquist Edgar Bergen and his dummy, Charlie McCarthy, and the Lone Ranger. Many of these shows offered children an opportunity to send in money for program gimmicks, such as Decoder Rings, much like one finds on cereal boxes today. This proved to be quite successful with young radio patrons and helped to advertise the show's products.

Relate

Visit the local community library or bookstore to locate an audio tape of any of these early radio shows from the 1930s and 1940s. Listen to them. Work with a group of peers to create your own weekly radio broadcast using any of the popular drama, comedy, or game show formats. Offer a program gimmick as part of your marketing plan. Perform your broadcast for classmates over the school's public address system much like a radio broadcast where listeners cannot see you but can only hear you in action.

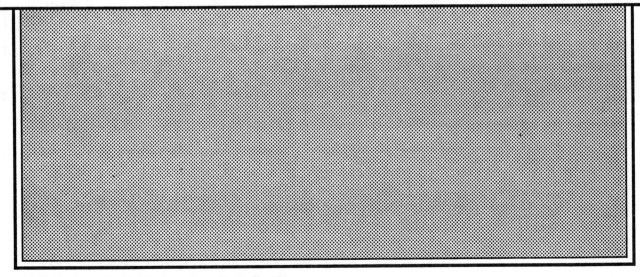

Laws, Lawbreakers, And Law Trials To Argue About

COMMUNICATION

Read

There are many weird and wacky laws that still exist on the lawbooks today because they have never been repealed by lawmakers over time. Some of these crazy laws are:
1. In California, it is against the law to enter a restaurant on a horse.
2. In Kentucky, it is against the law to carry an ice-cream cone in your pocket.
3. In Missouri, it is against the law to auction off your turtle.
4. In Utah, it is against the law to hitch your bike to an airplane.

Relate

Choose one or more of these weird and wacky laws and invent a tall tale to explain "how and why" it became a law. Use your imagination and write down your story for others to read and enjoy. Use the law itself as the opening line to your tall tale creation.

Read

History has produced many infamous crooks and criminals. "Billy the Kid," born in 1859, was very young and very small in stature. He was a wild robber, gunslinger, and cattle rustler of the Old West. "Scarface Capone," born in 1899, was a leader of organized crime in New York City. He was famous for his "bootlegging" of liquor from Canada to the United States. The liquor was secretly sold in popular bars, or "speakeasies," during Prohibition.

Relate

Design a "WANTED POSTER" for one or more of the notorious lawbreakers described here. Be sure your poster includes a short, but descriptive, paragraph outlining the historical background of this crooked individual. Hang it in the CLASSROOM CROOKS HALL OF SHAME.

Laws, Lawbreakers, And Law Trials To Argue About

COMMUNICATION

Read

In the Dred Scott vs. Sanford (1857) court case, an army surgeon, Dr. John Emerson, moved from a slave state to a free state, and took his slave, Dred Scott, with him during these moves. After Sanford's death, Dred Scott sued the wife of John Emerson for his freedom. The Court ruled that slaves were property like farm animals and therefore could not be free citizens of any state.

In the Brown vs. Board of Education (1954) court case, it was ruled that Linda Brown (a young African-American) of Topeka, Kansas, could attend a white school close to home instead of an all-black school almost two miles away. This decision led to desegregation of schools.

In the Roe vs. Wade (1973) court case, "Jane Roe" (a fictitious name) sued the state of Texas to allow her to have an abortion which was not legal at the time. The Supreme Court ruled in her favor, and to this day abortion is one of the most controversial legal topics still under debate.

Relate

Research to find out more details and information about one of these famous trials. Pretend you are a reporter assigned to cover the trial events. Write a feature or news story about the trial, discussing the major issues.

Without The Love Of Books, The Richest Man Is Poor

COMMUNICATION

Read

Every year important awards are given to authors of children's books. Some of these are:

- The Caldecott Medal, given by the American Library Association, for the best illustrated book;
- The Newbery Medal, given by the American Library Association, for the most distinguished American children's literature;
- The Horn Book Award, given by the Boston Globe, for the most outstanding juvenile books in the U.S. (fiction, nonfiction, and illustration); and
- The Coretta Scott King Award, given by the American Library Association, for authors and illustrators whose books promote the contributions of all people to the American dream.

Relate

Pretend that you are giving a prestigious award each year to an author who writes fiction or nonfiction books for readers of your age. What would you call the award? What would the award look like or be? Who would receive the award for this school year?

Read

Storybook characters often become friends of their readers over generations. They appear to be timeless in that they are enjoyed and remembered long after one becomes an adult. Some popular characters you may be familiar with are: Alice, Amelia Bedelia, Charlie, Charlotte, Claudia, Dorothy, Eloise, Encyclopedia Brown, Fudge, Hans Brinker, Harriet, Homer Price, Laura, Madeline, Mafatu, Nancy Drew, Pippi, Ramona, and Tom Sawyer.

Relate

Create a game that focuses on famous storybook characters using a format that is familiar to you and your friends. Consider board games, card games, television games, or word games in your design.

Without The Love Of Books, The Richest Man Is Poor

COMMUNICATION

Read

Melvil Dewey, an American librarian who lived from 1851 to 1931, became so upset when he tried to help people find books on unlabeled shelves of the library that he invented the Dewey Decimal System of Classification, which is still used in libraries today. This system numbers books by their subject matter, and is organized like this:

900 - General, Geography, History and Their Auxiliaries
800 - Literature
700 - The Arts
600 - Technology
500 - Pure Sciences
400 - Language
300 - Social Sciences
200 - Religion
100 - Philosophy and Related Disciplines
000 - Generalities

Relate

Use the Dewey Decimal System to locate a picture book for each of the categories in the Dewey Decimal System. Read each book and design an informative book mark that summarizes the content of each book similar to those that are given away with purchases at popular retail book stores.

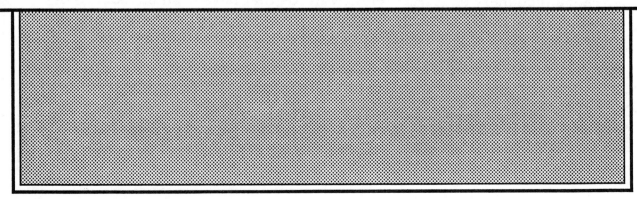

Language Lingo

COMMUNICATION

Read

There are over 3000 different languages spoken throughout the world today. One half of all the people in the world today speak one of 15 languages. More people in the world speak Mandarin Chinese than any other language.

Relate

Choose a popular phrase in English and research how to say and spell that phrase in at least five other languages.

Read

Language is always changing and new vocabulary is always emerging, depending upon world events and issues. For example, World War II introduced such words as "blitz" and "radar" while space travel introduced such words as "astronaut" and "blast-off."

Relate

Create a dictionary of at least ten new words that have been introduced or redefined as a result of a new event or set of happenings. Consider a dictionary of teen talk, of video game jargon, of military slang, of surfer words, or of computer age terminology.

Language
Lingo

Read

We refer to "dead languages" as languages that are no longer the native language of any living people. They are studied and understood only by scholars in universities, monasteries, and museums. Examples of "dead" languages are ancient Greek, Latin, Sanskrit, Gothic, Old Norse, and Old English.

Relate

Write a short story, skit, play, or poem about one of the following topics:
- The Language That Refused To Die
- The Language That Was Reborn Again
- The Language That Was Buried Alive
- The Language That Rose from the Dead
- The Language That Outsmarted the Natives

Sports, Games, And Clubs

SCHOOL CULTURE AND ACADEMIC SURVIVAL

Read

The Frisbee has been around for over 30 years and was invented by Fred Morrison after World War II. As a kid, Mr. Morrison had thrown pie tins into the air to watch them fly. His early metal discs were too heavy, so he turned to plastic for his flying toy. Today there are Frisbee clubs and tournaments all over the world.

Relate

Plan a Frisbee contest for your class. Publicize the date, time, and place as well as the rules for play and entry. Design awards, ribbons, or trophies for this event.

Read

Kites were first made in China more than 2500 years ago. Kites have been used in times of war to carry burning bombs over enemy territory, and they have been used to carry special instruments high into the sky to measure wind pressure and air temperature. Benjamin Franklin used a kite to prove that lightning was a kind of electricity.

Relate

Locate books on kite-making and flying in your school media center. Work with the art teacher to design mini-kites and hold a kite-flying field day for your class. Compose a haiku, diamante, limerick, concrete, or free verse poem about kites and mat these on a colored paper, kite-shaped background. Add a piece of string and hang them around the classroom for display.

Sports, Games, And Clubs

SCHOOL CULTURE AND ACADEMIC SURVIVAL

Read

Yo-Yos were first brought to the U.S. by Pedro Flores of the Philippines where kids had played with them for years. Donald F. Duncan bought Flores's company and improved upon the Flores design. The word "yo-yo" means "come-come" or "to return." Yo-yos are made with both wood and plastic.

Relate

Plan a "yo-yo" party for your class complete with invitations, decorations, food, how-to sessions for learning "yo-yo" tricks, and "yo-yo" events. Many novelty stores offer special quantity prices for purchasing large numbers of yo-yos for educational institutions. Check your yellow pages!

Read

Skateboards were most likely invented by surfers who wanted to practice surfing moves on land when the waves weren't any good. The first skateboards had clay or metal wheels which were dangerous, but these were later replaced with plastic wheels which gripped the ground far better than the earlier ones, making skateboarding a safer sport. Many schools have skateboard teams that compete with one another in an intrascholastic setting.

Relate

Conduct a survey of students in your class or school to determine who likes to skateboard, where and when they practice their skateboarding, and what type of skateboard they own. Graph your results. You might also want to plan a "skateboarding" show or demonstration by students who are experts at the sport. Work with the principal to plan and schedule a "skateboarding" exhibition on the school grounds.

Dealing With Natural Disasters

SCHOOL CULTURE AND ACADEMIC SURVIVAL

Read

A tornado is a noisy and dangerous windstorm that looks like a long funnel hanging down from a large, dark cloud. In a tornado, the wind whirls around in a circle and sucks up anything in its path. The whirling wind of a tornado can spin as fast as 28 miles per hour and can travel 20 to 40 miles an hour.

Relate

Write a children's book about a tornado that could be used to teach younger students about both the origin and the dangers of a tornado. Be sure to include a set of "tips" for protecting oneself against the onset of a tornado at home or at school.

Read

A hurricane is another type of windstorm that originates at sea. Like a tornado, a hurricane is made up of whirling winds, and it stretches across 300 to 400 miles at one time. Hurricane winds move at speeds ranging from 75 to 200 miles an hour and can cause huge waves on the ocean, heavy rains on land, and extensive flooding along the seashore.

Relate

Create a special television commercial to teach people about the origin and dangers of a hurricane. Make certain that your message also points out to the viewer what he or she can do in the event of a hurricane.

Dealing With Natural Disasters

SCHOOL CULTURE AND ACADEMIC SURVIVAL

Read

An earthquake is caused by the snapping or breaking of the earth's crust and can last anywhere from one to many minutes. Forces inside the earth are always squeezing and straining the rock of the earth's crust, but they don't always cause the rock to snap. Scientists aren't always sure why this happens, but they warn of the dangers of an earthquake when the ground begins to shake and shiver violently.

Relate

Pretend you are a reporter who is covering an earthquake in California. Write a feature story that tells readers what they need to know about the origin and dangers of an earthquake in case one should occur again.

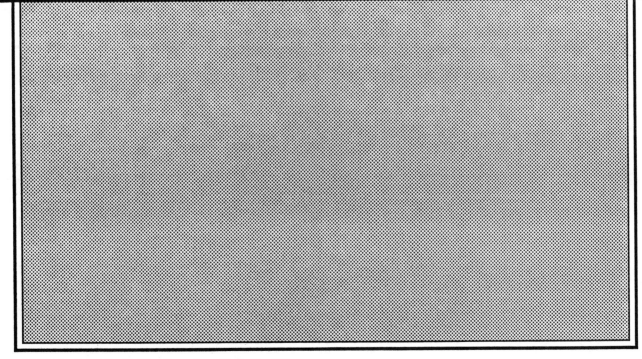

Record Breakers And Shakers

Read

The largest unit of money ever made in the United States was a $100,000 bill that bore the head of Salmon Portland Chase, the Secretary of the Treasury during the Civil War. None of these bills have been printed since 1955, and there are under 400 still in circulation today.

Relate

Pretend that a philanthropist gave your school a $100,000 bill to improve both its facility and program. Outline a plan for using this money to redesign both your school plant and grounds as well as classroom materials and methods.

Read

A man by the name of Robert Wadlow, who was born in Illinois in 1918, is the tallest person on record who ever lived. Robert was 6 feet tall by the time he was 8 years old and 7½ feet tall at the age of 15. He grew to be 8 feet 11 inches and weighed 491 pounds as an adult.

Relate

Pretend you are a talk show host for a popular radio station on a show entitled: "Record Breakers and Shakers." Stage an interview between yourself and Robert Wadlow when he was 8 years old and 7½ feet tall. What questions would you ask him and what problems would you expect him to have at home and at school?

Record Breakers And Shakers

SCHOOL CULTURE AND ACADEMIC SURVIVAL

Read

The highest number in math does not exist because all you have to do is add the number 1 to any number and you've got a higher number. The highest number that scientists have a name for is the centillion. It's a 1 followed by 600 zeros.

Relate

Think up a creative way to demonstrate infinity or explain a centillion.

Read

The world's fastest creature is a bird called the duck hawk, which can fly through the air at the speed of 180 miles per hour. The fastest creature on land is the cheetah, a large cat from the plains of Africa, which can run as fast as 70 miles an hour. There are fast swimming fish as well. One of these is the sailfish, which has been known to move in the water at the speed of 65 miles per hour.

Relate

Pretend you are the manufacturer of toy airplanes, boats, or automobiles and that you have just designed a new model that is "fast and furious." Name your product after the duck hawk, the cheetah, or the sailfish and develop a marketing plan complete with advertisements or commercials to promote it.

Famous Performances By Famous People

Read

Harry Houdini was a well-known trapeze artist, magician, and, ultimately, the world's greatest escape artist. His daring escapes were made after he had been handcuffed, chained, locked in a box, and suspended high in the air or sunk deep in the water. Houdini would manage to escape in seconds; few people understand the secrets of his success.

Relate

With a group of friends, plan and perform a magic show complete with tricks, costumes, and props.

Read

Phineas Taylor Barnum (better known as P.T. Barnum) was an expert at organizing exhibitions, shows, and theater performances. Whenever and wherever he could find an audience, he would prepare and put on a show. He began his career performing at fairgrounds, showing off unusual acts that involved such sights as dwarfs, talking animals, mermaids, and human freaks. He later started a touring circus billed as "The Greatest Show on Earth." This show became known as the "Barnum and Bailey Circus" after Barnum merged his show with that of James Bailey.

Relate

Consider organizing and putting on a classroom circus. When and where will it be? What souvenirs and refreshments will you offer? What acts and costumes will you have? What will you charge for tickets and other consumer items? What will the program look like?

Famous Performances By Famous People

SCHOOL CULTURE AND ACADEMIC SURVIVAL

Read

Bill Cosby is one of the world's greatest entertainers: he is a successful comedian, writer, movie actor, and television star. He also endorses many commercial products as an advertising spokesperson for major businesses and corporations. Cosby's humor often focuses on family life, and he says he receives most of his ideas from the experience of his poor childhood in Philadelphia and from his current family of wife, four daughters, and one son.

Relate

Try writing and producing a comedy show for your class, Bill Cosby-style. Think of several family situations that might lend themselves to a plot for a new situation comedy (sitcom) for television. Write the script, hold auditions for the character parts, and rehearse the scenes. Perform the comedy show and determine audience ratings.

Technological Wonders That Entertain

SCHOOL CULTURE AND ACADEMIC SURVIVAL

Read

Pinball machines use gravity to keep the pinball rolling. Because the table (the top of the pinball machine) is slanted, gravity pulls the ball toward the pit at the bottom of the table. To keep the ball in play, you must keep it away from the pit.

Relate

Design an original pinball machine based on a theme of your own choosing.

Read

Most audio tapes are a strip of plastic coated with a layer of rust. A tape recorder changes sound waves into electrical signals. A tape player changes the signals back into sound waves. Some machines can both record and play back sound.

Relate

Create an original audio tape to entertain others in your class. Consider making a tape of your favorite jokes and riddles, of your favorite limericks and puns, of your favorite anecdotes, or of your favorite raps.

Technological Wonders That Entertain

Read

Most video game systems are made of a base unit, game cartridges, and controls such as a joystick. The base unit holds a small computer. The computer uses microchips to work. One computer chip is the brain of the system. The brain chip is the microprocessor. Game cartridges plug into the base unit and each of these cartridges also has its own computer chips. These chips contain the computer programs that make up the game.

Relate

With your classmates, write reviews of your favorite video games much as you would write book and/or movie reviews. Stage a classroom demonstration of the top five video games as determined by the students in your class.

The Great Brain

Read

The brain is the largest and most important part of a person's nervous system. The human brain is about 3½ pounds of gray and white gelatin-like substance. It weighs only one-fiftieth as much as the body, yet it uses one-fourth of the blood's oxygen. The brain is an information storage space and a how-to library. It knows how to put facts and ideas together as well as how to figure out problems.

Relate

Create a booklet of "brain-teaser" problems for others to solve.

Read

The brain is also a drugstore that fills its prescriptions in split seconds. When you are hurt, for example, the brain sends out a chemical called "enkephalin" which is a pain-killer. When you encounter a potential danger, the brain sends a chemical called "norepinephrine" through your body which in turn starts another chemical called "adrenaline" flowing to warn you of danger.

Relate

The brain is said to be the "computer" of the body. Compare and contrast the brain with a computer. How are they alike and how are they different? Show your ideas in a comic strip or cartoon format.

The Great Brain

Read

The brain is a message center, too. It's like a big telephone exchange with messages coming in and out all the time. Each second the brain receives more than 100 million nerve messages from your body, and it knows what to do with them.

Relate

Design your own message pads, stationery, or memo slips for sending communications to one another in the classroom. Can you include a "brainy" graphic, symbol, or slogan as part of your design?

Featuring Your Physical Self

SELF-CONCEPT AND RELATIONSHIPS

Read

A "funny bone" is a nerve at the back of your elbow close to the bone. When you hit your funny bone, you get a painful tingling feeling in your arm.

Relate

Browse through the local newspaper to locate an article that causes a "painful tingling feeling" in your head or your heart.

Read

Wisdom teeth do not make you smarter. They are simply the last four teeth that come into your mouth and that are located in the farthest back position of your mouth. People don't get them until they are teenagers or young adults. Because they appear at so late an age, people call them wisdom teeth.

Relate

Think of someone you know in a leadership role. Give that person a few "words of wisdom" on how to perform his or her role or job better.

Featuring Your Physical Self

SELF-CONCEPT AND RELATIONSHIPS

Read

A "charley horse" is not a horse at all but a kind of a muscle cramp which is caused by too much exercise that makes a muscle work too hard. When you overextend a muscle, it tightens up and causes a sharp pain. Resting the muscle and keeping it warm will help the muscle to relax again.

Relate

Develop a simple exercise program that could be done in the classroom to relieve stress and boredom between classes or assignments.

Read

Goose pimples are tiny bumps that sometimes come out of your skin when you are either cold or frightened. If you look closely at the bumps, you will see a tiny hair in the center of each one which is held in place by a tiny muscle. When you get scared or chilled, each of these muscles tightens up to make little bumps. We call these goose pimples because they look just like the bumps on the skin of a plucked goose!

Relate

What social problem or issue in today's world most frightens you and causes you to become cold with goose bumps when you think about it? Discuss this problem or issue with a friend.

Your Rights, Needs, And The Law

SELF-CONCEPT AND RELATIONSHIPS

Read

The United Nations made a formal declaration of children's rights in 1959. The purpose of this action was to guarantee life, liberty, and the pursuit of happiness for children all over the world. The list of rights was designed to meet the physical and personal needs of children during their developmental years.

Relate

Create a banner, bumper sticker, and flag promoting children's rights in your school.

Read

There are also laws in many states or countries that protect children under the age of 18 in the workplace. In many places it is against the law for children to:
- work in places that sell or buy liquor
- ride or work on dangerous machines
- sell door to door
- sell things on the street
- work before 6:00 A.M. or after 7:00 P.M.
- work more than three hours a day

Usually, rules about working hours do not apply to such jobs as babysitting, delivering newspapers, mowing lawns, shoveling snow, and doing odd jobs in the neighborhood.

Relate

Create a résumé for yourself to use when applying for one of the following jobs: baby sitter, lawn caretaker, errand boy/girl, or party planner.

Your Rights, Needs, And The Law

SELF-CONCEPT AND RELATIONSHIPS

Read

According to the United Nations, children have the right to:
- enjoy the rights listed regardless of race, color, sex, religion, or nationality
- grow up in a healthy and normal way that is free and dignified
- a name and nationality
- social security that includes a decent place to live, a safe place to play, and a place to receive health care
- special treatment and schooling if handicapped
- love and understanding from parents or guardians
- free schooling and an opportunity to become everything they can be
- prompt protection and relief in times of disaster
- protection against all kinds of neglect, cruelty, and being used by others
- protection from any kind of unfair treatment because of race or religion

Relate

Design a series of greeting cards that could be sold to celebrate United Nations Children's Day each year.

Scientific Beliefs About The Future

SELF-CONCEPT AND RELATIONSHIPS

Read

Scientists believe that by the year 2000, most Americans will have a special leisure room in their homes that will contain a computerized entertainment system which is activated with a single switch or button. People will be able to turn their surroundings into a wide variety of scientific experiences ranging from an underground cave in New Mexico to a space colony on Mars. They will also be able to simulate what it is like to pilot a jet across the world or go hang gliding from a mountain top in California.

Relate

Draw a picture of a science-related setting that you would like to be able to simulate in your family room at home.

Read

Scientists predict that people will be wearing special clothing made out of a synthetic fabric that will never wear out and that will contain an automatic temperature control so that the person can adjust his or her clothing for comfort whether living at the North Pole or in the Sahara Desert.

Relate

Pretend you are a fashion designer of the future who specializes in fabrics that automatically adjust to the wearer's environment. Create a series of fashion outfits for a Paris Designer Show.

Scientific Beliefs About The Future

SELF-CONCEPT AND RELATIONSHIPS

Read

Scientists predict that by the year 2020, anti-aging drugs will be available for patients upon demand. People will be able to have considerable control over their projected life span and their growth rates or patterns.

Relate

Pretend you have been asked by the U.S. government to develop the Department of Controlled Aging. The job of this agency will be to establish rules and guidelines for administering treatment and prescriptions to individuals who want to postpone the aging process. Because the world's population is getting too large, the Department of Controlled Aging must establish a "grow old gracefully" program that is equitable to all citizens of this country. Under what rules or guidelines will you operate?

Animal Stereotypes
That Just Aren't True

SELF-CONCEPT AND RELATIONSHIPS

Read

It has been said that the males of many animal species do not take fatherhood seriously and often abandon their mates shortly after the birth of their offspring. This simply isn't true for many creatures. The male catfish, for example, carries the eggs of his offspring in his mouth for two months before the eggs hatch, and the male toad balances the eggs he fertilizes on his hind legs and takes them into the water regularly to keep them moist!

Relate

Write a humorous scientific report that discusses the dilemma of a male catfish who develops a sore throat during the two months before his offspring are to hatch or a report that records the problem of the male toad who is afraid of the water.

Read

Many uninformed persons feel that Mother Nature does not have adequate protection from her enemies, especially that of man. This simply is not true. Did you know, for example, that the poisonous mushroom called the "death cap" sends those who eat it into fits of vomiting and delirium that kill 90% of them within 15 hours and that the "golden dart-poison frog" of South America carries enough venom to kill nearly 1500 people when used on the ends of darts carried by South American Indians?

Relate

Write an historical account for a social studies textbook of two unusual wars that were fought and won by groups of people who took advantage of the "death cap" and the "golden dart-poison frog" as the major source of their weaponry.

Animal Stereotypes That Just Aren't True

SELF-CONCEPT AND RELATIONSHIPS

Read

People sometimes don't realize how creatures of differing species in nature become partners in their survival over time. The tickbird and the rhinoceros, for example, are friends because the tickbird likes to eat the ticks buried in the rhino's thick hide, and the rhino is more than happy to get rid of these bothersome pests. Similarly, the sea anemone is often attached to the outside of a hermit crab's shell. The crab carries the anemone around and shares its food while the anemone hides the crab among its stinging tentacles and attacks any enemies that threaten their well-being.

Relate

Write a short news clip for a mock television show about nature that teaches young children about the magic and mysteries of the animal world.

Language And Word Origins

Read

Most scholars believe language originated very slowly, beginning with grunts, barks, and hoots. Language makes it possible for people to communicate through written and oral means.

Relate

Try this: Communicate with your friends during lunch without using formal language. Record what happens!

Read

Music is one of the oldest arts. People probably began singing as soon as language developed. The first musical instruments were undoubtedly hunting tools being struck together.

Relate

Use kitchen utensils to perform an original or favorite piece of music. Enjoy!

Language And Word Origins

SELF-CONCEPT AND RELATIONSHIPS

Read

Every word was once a poem. Each began as a picture. Our language is made up of terms that were all originally figures of speech. To know the history of a word makes its present meaning clearer and more interesting. Playing with words can be entertaining and adventuresome. Try it—you'll like it!

Relate

It's fun to create jokes about names of people. These jokes involve puns or a "play on words." Study the examples of name jokes below and then try thinking up some of your own.

Q: Who started his own taxi service in Hong Kong?
A: Rick Shaw

Q: What man delivers cargo from one state to another?
A: Mack Truck

Q: Who has the most powerful weapons in space?
A: Ray Gun

Exploring Social Customs Through Celebrations

SELF-CONCEPT AND RELATIONSHIPS

Read

People in Japan celebrate Buddha's birthday with a flower festival on April 8th. Buddha was a great religious leader in India who taught people to be kind and thoughtful to one another. On Buddha's birthday the Japanese Buddhist children go to their local temples dressed in floral silk kimonos (robes) carrying fresh flowers. Many floats pass by in a parade, and one float always carries a statue of Buddha on a huge white elephant.

Relate

Design a flower float that might be used in the Buddha's birthday parade. To do this, use an old shoe box and cover it on all sides with paint, wrapping paper, or cloth. Create objects to put on the top of your float that will depict the theme of flowers, peace, and kindness.

Read

People in England celebrate Pancake Day on Shrove Tuesday, the day before Lent begins. Many years ago Christians were not supposed to eat fats, milk, and eggs during Lent, so they used up these foods to make pancakes before Lent began. On Pancake Day the kids play "toss-the-pancake" and hold "pancake races" whereby participants must flip the pancake out of the frying pan at least three times during the race.

Relate

Stage a Pancake Day for your class. Make and serve pancakes as refreshments and stage "pancake-related" games for entertainment. You might even want to make a recipe book of favorite "pancake recipes" with all types of variations.

Exploring Social Customs Through Celebrations

SELF-CONCEPT AND RELATIONSHIPS

Read

French Canadians who live in Quebec celebrate Jean Baptiste Day on June 24th with a parade. Jean Baptiste, St. John the Baptist, was the patron saint of Quebec. He is often shown in pictures as a little boy dressed like a shepherd. Often a lamb with a ribbon and bow around its neck stands next to St. John. During this eight-day festival, the French Canadians in Quebec honor the French language and culture.

Relate

Research important facts about Quebec and the French culture in that region. Create a series of commemorative plates honoring the special people, places, and events discovered through your research. You can use paper plates and crayons or magic markers to create your own designs for the occasion.

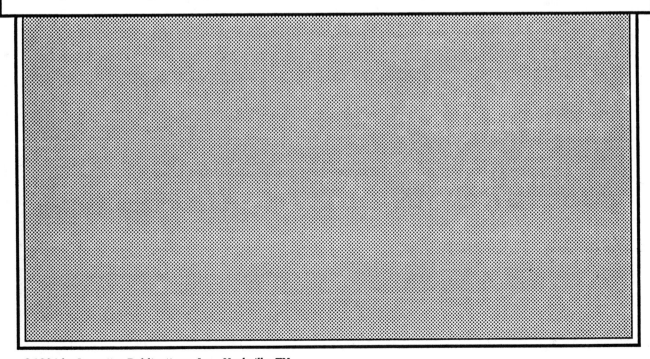

The Calendar: Responsibility For Time

PROBLEM-SOLVING AND DECISION-MAKING

Read

The word "calendar" is derived from the Roman word "kalenda" which means the first of the month. Julius Caesar is credited with the development of the calendar year based on 365¼ days in a solar year with one extra day added every fourth year to make "leap year."

Relate

If you had to abolish one month from the year, what month would you choose and why?

Read

In the days before Julius Caesar, the sun was the major tool for measuring time. Charts, graphs, and journals were kept by hand to document the days and nights.

Relate

If there were no calendars, how would things be different? Create a skit which shows several consequences of a life without calendars.

The Calendar: Responsibility For Time

PROBLEM-SOLVING AND DECISION-MAKING

Read

The stars have had a significant impact on the evolution of the calendar. The first serious students of the stars were the ancient Babylonians. They began keeping accurate records of what happened in the sky over 5,000 years ago, and they were able to use their discoveries to create accurate calendars.

Relate

Design a series of drawings, cartoon style, that show what a calendar might say to the Big Dipper, a sun dial, a stopwatch, and a date book.

Read

February is the shortest month of the year, even during Leap Year (which occurs every fourth year). Even though it has the fewest number of days of any month, February has quite a number of special days to be observed and celebrated.

Relate

Pretend you are the February page of a monthly calendar. Write out a set of mathematical problems for the month of February. You might ask such questions as: (1) multiply the sum of the dates of each day in the third week of February by 189; (2) divide 2050 by the sum of the even dates in February; or (3) add the dates of every seventh day in February and multiply their total by the number of students in your classroom. Be sure to include an answer key.

Zest For Computers

PROBLEM-SOLVING AND DECISION-MAKING

Read

Programming means communicating with a computer in ways that it can understand. Using a code of letters, numbers, and symbols called programming language, you tell the computer what to do and how to do it. The machine changes the letters, numbers, and symbols into electrical pulses—its language.

Relate

Write a story with one of the following titles:
- "A Chip That Made a Mistake"
- "An Impulse That Took a Detour"
- "A Memory Who Caught Amnesia"
- "The Monitor Who Failed To Answer"
- "The Bilingual Printer"

Read

Computers use electricity to do their many jobs, and they work fast. In a second, a computer can do an amount of arithmetic that would keep 20 people busy all day.

Relate

Write a letter to the editor telling how a robot replaced you on your job at a fast-food restaurant, and write a letter to the editor explaining how computers have helped you find work after school.

Zest For Computers

PROBLEM-SOLVING AND DECISION-MAKING

Read

Michael Jackson put on an electrifying performance during his 1984 Victory Tour. As Jackson sang, computers controlled many of the show's special effects. One computer made a pair of robot spiders wriggle as the band performed. Another computer directed a laser-light show. Four other computers worked the lighting and sound systems.

Relate

Write a mock concert review of Michael Jackson's 2000 Victory Tour, discussing its new uses of computers in the performance.

Read

Xanada, a house near Orlando, Florida, is a house of tomorrow. The outside looks like something from another planet with its hardened plastic form that was sprayed onto huge balloons to form rooms. Inside, computers attached to dozens of electronic gadgets run everything from an automatic clothes retrieval system in the closet to the electronic tutor who selects your meals and daily activities.

Relate

Create a magazine layout for *Better Homes and Gardens* or *Architectural Digest* on Xanada, showing sketches (along with informative paragraphs) on the special features of the teen recreation room and the kids' dormitory bedrooms of this futuristic home.

Risk-Taking Myths And Mysteries

PROBLEM-SOLVING AND DECISION-MAKING

Read

Mermaids are mythical beasts, said to live in the sea, whose purpose is to use their lovely voices to lure sailors to their deaths by drowning. A mermaid's body is half woman and half fish with scales and a tail. Walt Disney Studios has created "The Little Mermaid" movie and figures to entertain young children all over the world.

Relate

Design an underwater house for a family of mermaids that could be used by young children in the bathtub, the swimming pool, or at the beach.

Read

Unicorns are also mythical beasts which were popular with the ancient Greeks and Romans. These creatures are said to look like a horse with a long, straight, spiral horn extending out from its forehead. In the Middle Ages, the unicorn was a symbol of purity and was often used by Christian artists when painting the Virgin Mary.

Relate

Design a piece of jewelry whose main figure is based on the concept of the unicorn.

Risk-Taking Myths And Mysteries

Read

Dragons are another popular mythical beast—although different people have different ideas about what they look like and whether they are good or bad. Most people think of dragons as having a body like a snake, wings like a bat, and a mouth like an alligator that breathes fire.

Relate

Design a coloring/activity book based on the theme of dragons. Include pictures to color, puzzles, mazes, follow-the-dot pages, pattern pages for making puppets, and masks, as well as dragon jokes and riddles.

Read

Monsters are another prehistoric mythical character. The Loch Ness Monster, for example, is said to be a gigantic water animal that lives in northern Scotland at the bottom of a long and deep lake called Loch Ness. Many travelers to Loch Ness claim they have seen this monster rising from the lake.

Relate

Design a children's picture book about the Loch Ness Monster who turns out to be a good friend rather than a bad creature.

Working With Chocolate

PROBLEM-SOLVING AND DECISION-MAKING

Read

Chocolate chip cookies were first patented by the Toll House Inn outside of Whitman, Massachusetts. The inn's cook and owner, Mrs. Ruth Wakefield, decided to put chocolate pieces from a large Nestle's chocolate bar into her regular cookie dough to make it taste better for her customers. The owners of Nestle's decided to put this recipe on the back of their candy bar, and when it became extremely popular they decided to manufacture packages of these chocolate bits.

Relate

Create an original wrapping paper design with matching greeting card that could be used to gift wrap a box of homemade chocolate chip cookies. Make up a batch of chocolate chip cookies, and wrap them in your new paper. Give your present to a special friend or adult.

Read

Chocolate sundaes originated in 1890 when a customer of E.C. Berner's ice-cream parlor in a small town of rural New York poured chocolate over a scoop of plain ice cream on a Sunday afternoon. Since this treat was more expensive than plain ice cream and was available only on Sundays, it was named after the seventh day of the week.

Relate

Arrange for your class to host an ice-cream sundae break on a Friday afternoon. Provide a wide assortment of chocolate toppings (such as chocolate sprinkles, chocolate chips, etc.) for this event.

Working With Chocolate

PROBLEM-SOLVING AND DECISION-MAKING

Read

Candy bars made out of chocolate tend to dominate the "sweet" snack food market. The Mars Bar was created by a Minnesota confectioner named Franklin Mars, who also invented the Milky Way, the Snickers Bar, and the 3 Musketeers Bar. Franklin Mars went on to create the popular M & M's to accommodate soldiers during World War II who wanted a small, but tasty treat that would "melt in their mouths and not in their hands."

Relate

Invent a new candy bar or packaged candy for the 21st century that is intended to be the "perfect" treat for today's busy family. Draw a large magazine ad that tells all about your new chocolate product using any of the popular propaganda techniques. Send your candy bar idea to a popular candy making manufacturer and ask for a reaction to your invention!

V Is For Virus

Read

A virus is smaller than the smallest bacteria that can be seen through an ordinary microscope. Viruses can multiply only within the living cells of humans, animal, or plants. Viruses are responsible for a wide range of infections, diseases, and illnesses.

Relate

Make up a short story of how a virus caused a major plague in history using a series of sequence cards to show the cause and effect.

Read

Antibiotics can be used to treat many diseases in both animals and humans. These drugs attack microorganisms called bacteria which are the cause of many infections. Although antibiotics work well against bacteria, they have almost no effect against viruses which are the other common cause of infection.

Relate

Design a get-well card for a sick virus from a well bacteria.

V Is For Virus

Read

Infection takes place when an organism is invaded by harmful bacteria and viruses which multiply in the organism and often cause severe damage. These invaders can enter a human being through many routes such as through the mouth when we eat contaminated food, through the skin when we endure a dirty cut or abrasion, or through the lungs when we breathe unclean air.

Relate

What might a virus say to a plate of spoiled meat, the dirty blade of a Boy Scout jackknife, or the polluted air of a garbage dump? Write your conversations in a series of "balloons."

Read

Viruses of a different type are also found in the world of technology and are called computer viruses. They can infiltrate complex data systems and destroy important files stored on computer disks.

Relate

Compose a short newspaper article telling about a terrible computer virus that was a big problem because it was "eating up" student records of the local school system.

Sex, Suicide, And Substance Abuse

PROBLEM-SOLVING AND DECISION-MAKING

Read

"Every 64 seconds . . . a baby is born to a teenage mother in this country. Five minutes later, a baby will have been born to a teenager who already has a child. Ten hours later . . . more than 560 babies will have been born to teenagers in America. Adolescent pregnancy, which for too many young people begins or perpetuates a cycle of poverty, remains a crisis in America." Source: Children's Defense Fund, *The State of America's Children, 1992* (Washington, D.C., 1992).

Relate

Host a panel discussion of adolescent mothers. Ask them a series of questions to help you better understand the issues and realities of teenage pregnancies. Then work in small groups to generate a list of potential and probable outcomes of an unwanted pregnancy for you and/or your friends. Classify the items on your list as having a positive or negative impact on your life. What conclusions can you draw from this exercise?

Read

While we are bombarded with information and cues about the harm of substance abuse, we are also faced with a constant stream of advertising messages that glamorize the world of cigarettes, alcohol, and drugs. These ads make chemicals seem an acceptable way to handle life's problems. One thing, though, is for certain. Intoxication by any substance is not acceptable, and there are more constructive ways for you to meet your personal needs.

Relate

Create a series of "Fact Sheets" about the dangers of alcohol and drugs. Include information about the effects on the body's organs and the effects on the individual's pocketbook. Use these fact sheets to do one or more of these activities:

1. Create a series of skits that could be performed for younger students.
2. Write a series of "raps" that could be taught to groups of younger students.
3. Invent a trivia game that could be played with younger students.

Sex, Suicide, And Substance Abuse

PROBLEM-SOLVING AND DECISION-MAKING

Read

Since 1960, the rate at which teenagers take their own lives has more than tripled. Suicide is now the second leading cause of death among adolescents. For every successful suicide there are at least 50 to 100 adolescent suicide attempts. Furthermore, because of the social stigma associated with suicide, many deaths that are said to be accidents are actually due to suicide.

Source: Edward Ziglar, *Children: Developmental and Social Issues*, 1988; S. M. Finch and E. D. Poznaski, *Adolescent Suicide*, 1971; P. C. Hollinger, "Adolescent Suicide: An Epidemiological Study of Recent Trends," *American Journal of Psychiatry*, 1978.

Relate

Inability to communicate and interact constructively with peers of the opposite sex is one reason early adolescents think about suicide as a solution to their problems. Young people rarely take time to dialogue with one another about things they have in common or focus on the differences that make them unique or special. Arrange for social times in your school week when kids can talk about themselves with one another. Use a set of structured questions during these classroom sessions to encourage positive interaction. Some examples are listed below. Compile a list of additional questions.

1. What do you think would be the most surprising difference if you could change sexes for one day?
2. Do you think boys or girls have it easier in today's world?
3. What is the worst (or best) "pick-up" line you have ever heard?
4. Do you believe in love at first sight?
5. What quality do you most admire in people of the opposite sex? Of your sex?
6. How would you break off a relationship of no more interest to you?
7. Who is your best friend of the opposite sex?
8. What social event of mixed company have you attended that you hated to go to but ended up having a good time?
9. Are you basically an affectionate person? Explain.
10. Do you act differently when you are in groups of mixed company than you do when you are only with people of your sex? Why or why not?

APPENDIX

Ready-To-Use Thematic Activities To Accommodate Differing Learning Styles

Independent Study Format
(Communications)

Structured Learning Center Format
(School Culture and Academic Survival)

Mini Unit Format
(Self-Concept and Relationships)

Free Choice Learning Center
(Problem-Solving and Decision-Making)

Organizational Chart for Multi-Grade Grouping

Other Incentive Publications Materials Related to Interdisciplinary Instruction: An Annotated Bibliography

Index

Independent Study To Accommodate Differing Learning Styles

ART FOR ART'S SAKE

(Art as a Means of Communication)

Make a survey of the art books in your school library. Write a critical analysis of the books available, paying particular attention to their contribution to multicultural and historical understandings.

Study several tessellations (in books, posters, or magazines) and then design one of your own to convey a message or an emotion. After the design is finished, color it to give it added meaning.

Create a classroom junk sculpture (made from paper clips, crayon pieces, chalk, cardboard or paper scraps, rubber bands, etc.) that carries a message of social importance (for example, world peace, world unity, friendship, harmony, conservation of natural resources, etc.). You may decide to make a detailed sketch of such a sculpture instead.

Select a well-known painter whose work you admire. Study the artist's style as reflected in several of his or her works. Then experiment to try to imitate the basic style and techniques used in the artist's work to gain a better understanding of the artist's techniques (broad, sweeping strokes; pointillism; fine details; etc.).

Independent Study To Accommodate Differing Learning Styles

ART FOR ART'S SAKE

(Art as a Means of Communication)

Fingerpaint or do a crayon scribble drawing to a classical recording to portray your interpretation of the feelings and emotions expressed through the music.

Work with a partner to study the life and works of a contemporary artist in order to write a feature article for the Sunday magazine section of a nationally distributed newspaper.

Develop a graphic scrapbook of your life and times. Use sketches, drawings, cartoons, and comics to show the major events in your life to date. Begin with your earliest memories. Your graphic autobiography may reveal a more interesting person than you had previously envisioned.

COMPUTER COUNTDOWN

A Learning Center Designed To Accommodate Seven Differing Learning Styles

Objective:

The student will gain increased awareness and understanding of the significance of the role of computers in his or her school.

Major Content Focus:

Social Studies

Interdisciplinary Content Strands:

Language/Writing; Graphics/Drawing; Math; Science; Music/Drama; Research

Verbal/Linguistic

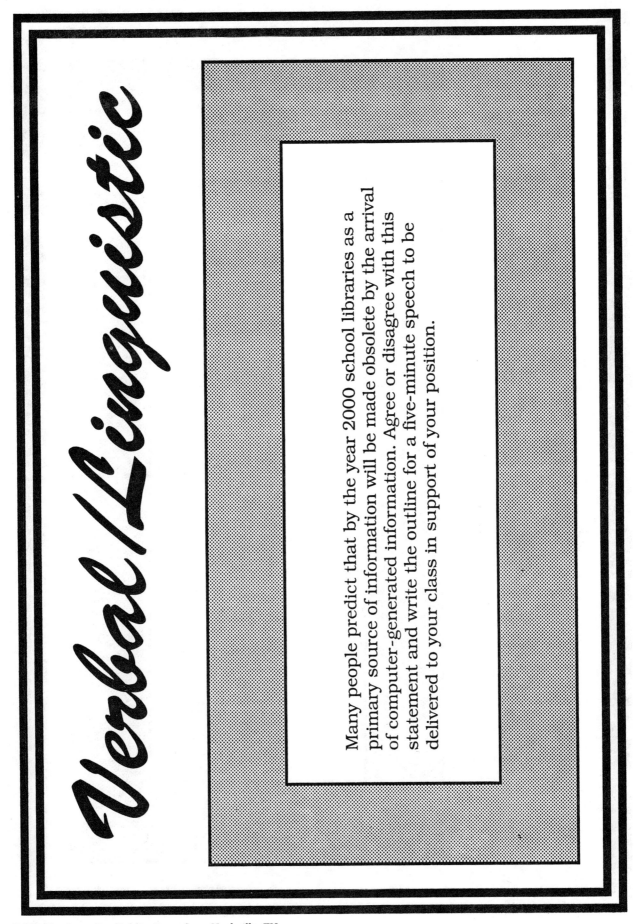

Many people predict that by the year 2000 school libraries as a primary source of information will be made obsolete by the arrival of computer-generated information. Agree or disagree with this statement and write the outline for a five-minute speech to be delivered to your class in support of your position.

Visual/Spatial

Design a poster to show how computers are used in your school to improve the quality of student instruction.

Logical/Mathematical

Rank order the different ways in which computers are used in your school according to their importance in an average school day (for example, in scheduling, student instruction, graphic arts, record keeping, etc.).

Body/Kinesthetic

Create and act out a "human sculpture drama" for one of the following titles:

- The Dance of the Under-Powered Computer Keyboard
- The Dance of the Over-Powered Computer Keyboard
- Charades of the Computer Symbols Representing "Save," "Print," and "Delete"

Musical/Rhythmic

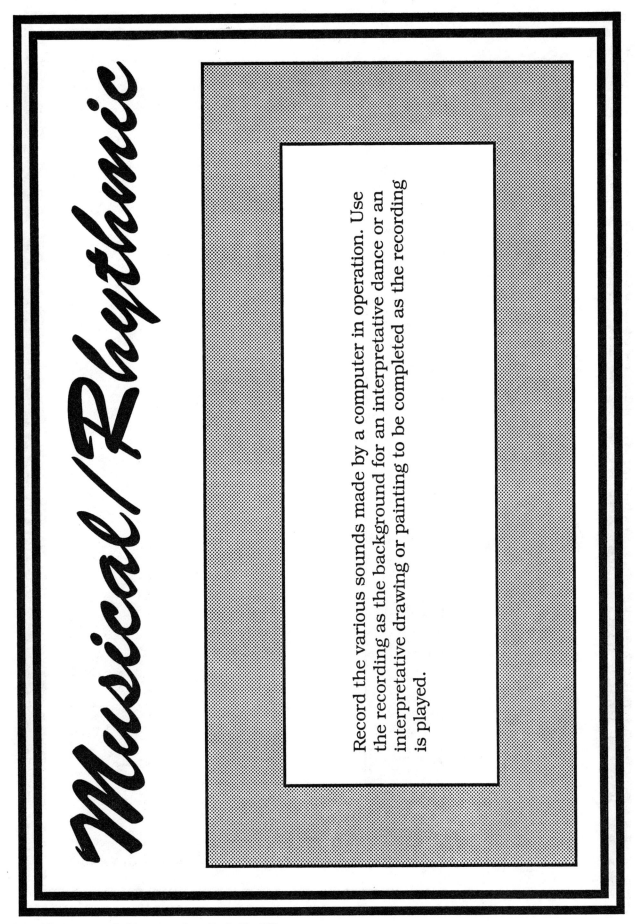

Record the various sounds made by a computer in operation. Use the recording as the background for an interpretative dance or an interpretative drawing or painting to be completed as the recording is played.

Interpersonal

Brainstorm and prioritize ways in which additional computers could be utilized in new, more creative or nontraditional means in your school.

Intrapersonal

Write down and analyze ways in which each and every computer in your school influences your daily life in school.

Verbal/Linguistic

Gather the information necessary to write an information manual for the proper care and maintenance of the computers in your school. Organize the information into a practical and easy-to-use format.

Logical/Mathematical

Estimate the cost of all the computers in your school. Research the subject to gain information necessary to determine the accuracy of your estimate.

Visual/Spatial

Gather information necessary to create a brochure to raise funds for additional computers for use in your school's instructional program. Then create the brochure.

Body/Kinesthetic

Plan and carry out a "computer awareness day" for your class. Include demonstrations, lecturettes, hands-on learning labs, etc.

OPTIONAL RESEARCH CHALLENGES

Musical/Rhythmic

Create or simulate a series of raps or sing-alongs to promote awareness of the value of your school's computer program.

Interpersonal

Cooperate with a partner to design a new computer game. Compare and contrast computer games with other recreational options that can be completed in the same time frame as a computer game.

OPTIONAL RESEARCH CHALLENGES

Intrapersonal

Analyze the importance of your school's computer program to your plans or hopes for life as an adult wage earner. Write a summary of your analysis.

Additional Questions To Find Answers For

1. How many teachers in your school are computer literate? How many own and use personal computers?

2. When were computers first introduced as a regular part of your school's curriculum? Trace the history of their use in your school.

3. Where does the money for your school's computers and their maintenance come from and who administers the expenditure?

4. How (and in what areas) do computers contribute to the school's enrichment and extracurricular activities?

5. Are students encouraged to use computers as a regular part of their daily lives? What measures are taken by the faculty to help them acquire the skills necessary to do so?

6. How are school-owned computers used after school hours and during school vacations and breaks? List other ways the computers could be used during these times.

7. How does the school's computer instructional program compare to that of other schools in the community as it relates to preparation for future academic success?

8. Compile a list of professions that require a knowledge of computers. What kind of education and training do these careers require?

9. Explore the technology of the CD-ROM. Write an essay describing three ways that CD-ROM technology could benefit your school's computer program. Provide specific examples.

10. Write an essay telling how computers have made your life both easier and more difficult. Emphasize whether you like working on a computer or feel more comfortable using other technology to write, learn, and research.

Mini Unit To Accommodate Differing Learning Styles

TIME OUT

(Recreation and Free Time)

Make a list of the ten books that you would like to read on your next summer vacation. Rank order the books according to your interest in them.

Make a time line to show the history of your favorite sport.

Draw a cartoon or a series of sketches to show how you would spend your perfect Saturday.

Create a brand new game to play with three or four classmates to relieve boredom or release tension.

Mini Unit To Accommodate Differing Learning Styles

TIME OUT

(Recreation and Free Time)

Use pencils, rulers, erasers and/or other classroom tools to create a tune to use as a springboard for discussion, pantomime, or an original game.

Teach someone whose company you enjoy to play a board game or ask that person to teach you a game that you do not know how to play.

Write a journal entry for today, highlighting the "free time activity" that you enjoyed the most. Think about why this activity was especially interesting and/or rewarding to you and write a brief summary of your feelings about it.

Learning About Learning Styles

You already know that each one of us is unique! We have different colored skin and hair. We have different shapes to our eyes and faces. We have different measurements in our weights and heights.

Did you know, however, that we also have different ways of thinking, learning, and feeling? Although these differences are important, we must also recognize that there are some common characteristics that most students share when it comes to learning something new. Studies have identified four distinct learning styles:

- Some people learn best by finding out WHY things happen or work as they do. IS THIS YOU?
- Some people learn best by asking WHAT happens or works when learning takes place. IS THIS YOU?
- Some people learn best by examining HOW things happen or work. IS THIS YOU?
- Some people learn best by discovering the IF in things that happen or work. IS THIS YOU?

Researchers have discovered that we are complex creatures with one dominant learning style and several back-up learning styles. It is important that we practice using all of these learning techniques if we are to become a "whole" person as an adult.

The following study projects have been planned to give you some practice in choosing varied approaches to learning more about yourself, your world, and your relationships with others. You may also discover that you can have fun while learning too!

Let's Do Lunch

Select items from the following "menu" to create your own "learning style feast." For a balanced menu, you will need to choose one item from each course:

- **APPETIZERS** *(starters)*
- **ENTREES** *(main courses)*
- **DESSERTS** *(sweet treats)*
- **CONDIMENTS** *(a little something extra)*

When you have made your selections, write them in the space below to create a customized plan of study!

Appetizers

Entrees

Desserts

Condiments

Date Project Started _____ Date Project Completed _____

Signature _____

Appetizers

Thinking ahead, tell what you are likely to be eating for lunch . . .
- . . . next week.
- . . . next year.
- . . . ten years from now.

Design a poster to encourage wise use of the earth's food supply.

Write a letter to the staff of your school lunch room, expressing appreciation for the school lunches. Be descriptive!

Invent a new game to play at lunchtime. Name the game and write down its rules of play.

Describe what would happen if you skipped lunch entirely for ten days in a row. Write an essay describing your feelings and the physical changes that would take place in your body.

Imagine the effect on your school's academic program if the entire cafeteria staff walked out and could not be replaced for a month. How would this situation affect teacher morale? Write a diary entry from either a teacher's or student's point of view.

List the titles of three recordings by your favorite musical group that you would consider good background music for lunch. Find out whether you could buy the recordings and how much they would cost.

Entrees

Use one of the following story starters to write a creative story.
- I couldn't believe he took me to *that* restaurant.
- "Not beans again!" shouted the captain.
- Our picnic table was suddenly invaded by an army of giant red ants.
- One way or the other, this problem of the lunch box thieves must be settled!
- Our school lunch room is the last place in the world that you would have expected . . .

You have heard the expression "a meal fit for a king." Plan a five-course menu that you would like to serve to visiting royalty. Write out the full menu.

Make up a lunch menu for an ant, a grasshopper, and a frog.

Estimate the cost of providing lunch for an elephant for a week. Do research to check the accuracy of your estimate.

Design a menu for a last day of school celebration for your school's faculty. One catch—this luncheon has to be prepared, paid for, and served by the students.

Draw or paint a picture to show your favorite lunch.

Write a short paragraph to explain the difference between lunch and brunch.

Write down your lunch menus of the past three days. Analyze each food item to gauge how healthily you have been eating.

Look at the food pages of a local newspaper to gather information on the cost of food in your city. Create a Sunday lunch menu for your family and compute its cost.

Assess the time allotted in your school schedule for lunch. Rate it as adequate, just fine, or poor. Explain your answer.

Desserts

Plan an apple harvest celebration luncheon menu including appetizers, entrees, desserts, and condiments, using apples as the main ingredient.

You know about breakfast, brunch, and lunch. Make up a new meal to be called "crunch." Whom will you invite to crunch and what will you have to eat?

Make up a new recipe for your family using potatoes, onions, and cauliflower as the main ingredients.

Do research to find out what astronauts eat for lunch when in outer space.

Why do most people eat three meals a day? Which is the meal most often skipped? Is there a better number of meals to eat?

Make up riddles with lunch themes. For example, "You will usually find me between two pieces of bread with a slice of cheese, mustard or mayonnaise, and sometimes a pickle." Answer: a slice of ham.

Tell where you would go, whom you would take with you, and what you would have to eat if you could plan the picnic of your dreams.

Decide which is the most important meal of the day: breakfast, lunch, or dinner. Give three reasons to justify your decision.

Condiments

An old nursery rhyme goes like this:
  Jack Spratt could eat no fat.
  His wife could eat no lean.
  So between the two,
  They licked the platter clean.

Draw a picture to show Jack and his wife at lunch.

Conduct a survey of your classmates to find our how many of them ate a well-balanced, healthy lunch yesterday. Graph your results.

Just for fun, find out how many of your classmates like peanut butter and jelly sandwiches, how many prefer just peanut butter, how many prefer just jelly, and how many hate peanut butter and jelly altogether. Make a Venn diagram to show the results of your survey.

Find out what your teachers eat for lunch on Saturdays and Sundays. Make a circle graph to show how healthily they eat on their days off.

Role play a boisterous, jolly lunch hour in your school cafeteria. Role play a celebratory lunch with friends at your house. Role play an elegant lunch in an expensive restaurant with your favorite famous person. Which situation would you enjoy most?

Draw a comic strip or cartoon to portray a hilarious luncheon episode.

Make up a ballad about a lunchtime adventure.

Organizational Chart For Multi-Grade Grouping

COMMUNICATION

Organizational Chart For Multi-Grade Grouping

SCHOOL CULTURE AND ACADEMIC SURVIVAL

Organizational Chart For Multi-Grade Grouping

SELF-CONCEPT AND RELATIONSHIPS

INSTRUCTIONAL DELIVERY SYSTEM	LEVEL	PAGE #
Major Interdisciplinary Units		
Color My World	I	46-51
The Talents, Traditions, and Trademarks of Americana Over Time	II	52-57
What Insects Can Teach Us About Life	III	58-63
Mini Interdisciplinary Units		
We're All in This Together	I	120-121
Parents as People	I	122-123
As Time Goes By	I	124-125
Teamwork Is No Mystery to the Science World	II	126-127
A Career as a Scientist	II	128-129
Enjoying My Social Self Through Science	II	130-131
Kids Can Do Their Share	III	132-133
It's All in the Cards	III	134-135
Learning To Be Peacemakers	III	136-137
Learning Centers		
How's Your IQ (Innovation Quotient)?	I	188-192
Investigate a Road Map	II	193-197
Investigate a Baseball Card Collection	III	198-202
Read and Relate		
Featuring Your Physical Self	I	244-245
Your Rights, Your Needs, and the Law	I	246-247
Scientific Beliefs About the Future	II	248-249
Animal Stereotypes That Just Aren't True	II	250-251
Language and Word Origins	III	252-253
Exploring Social Customs Through Celebrations	III	254-255

Organizational Chart For Multi-Grade Grouping

PROBLEM-SOLVING AND DECISION-MAKING

Other Incentive Publications Materials Related To Interdisciplinary Instruction:

AN ANNOTATED BIBLIOGRAPHY

Blond, Geri and Doris Spivak. *Inventions and Extensions.* Nashville, TN: Incentive Publications, 1991.
> This unique resource taps into kids' natural curiosity about how things work. Each activity is based on a famous invention and its inventor. Motivational questions and high-interest extended activities will encourage students to think and create.

Catherall, Ed. *Stuck on Magnets.* Catherall, Ed and Bev McKay. *Dropping in on Gravity; Turning to Wheels.* McKay, Bev. *Ants and More Ants; Bird Watch; Dragons; Footworks; Our Prehistoric Ancestors; Owls, Great and Small; Pirates of Old; Time on the Line; Whale Alert.* Nashville, TN: Incentive Publications, 1992.
> These high-interest thematic activities and projects are based on high-quality research. Each interdisciplinary unit offers a different approach that can nurture a variety of learning styles with activities drawn from the areas of language, social studies, math, and science.

Cochran, Judith. *Insights To Literature: Middle Grades.* Nashville, TN: Incentive Publications, 1990.
> Ten widely-acclaimed pieces of literature are presented through reproducible units and teacher's guides. Units contain comprehension questions and activities for each book chapter along with journal-writing activities. Teacher's guides contain pre- and post-reading questions and activities that touch on all areas of the curriculum. All are correlated to Bloom's Taxonomy.

Cook, Shirley. *180 Days Around the World.* Nashville, TN: Incentive Publications, 1993.
> This book gives students an opportunity to learn about 180 of the world's most interesting countries, provinces, and states and the people who inhabit them, while using genuine research skills. Enticing global "mysteries" and reproducible activities stimulate learning through inquiry and multicultural exploration.

Cook, Shirley. *Story Journal.* Nashville, TN: Incentive Publications, 1990.
> Seventeen books provide themes for daily journal-writing activities. Each activity introduces new vocabulary words and thought-provoking writing stimulators. At the end of each unit are extended activities to integrate literature with the curriculum and to exercise creative thinking.

Farnette, Cherrie, Imogene Forte, and Barbara Loss. *Special Kids' Stuff, Rev. Ed.* Nashville, TN: Incentive Publications, 1989.
> This resource contains high-interest/low-vocabulary language units with learning experiences presented at three or more levels of difficulty to provide for individual needs. The activities are designed to be used to supplement regular reading programs or to encourage the learning disabled student.

Forte, Imogene. *One Nation, 50 States.* Nashville, TN: Incentive Publications, 1993.
> Fifty interdisciplinary units include high-interest activities, extended learning projects, and lessons to enhance higher-level thinking skills. Everything needed to complete the activities and lessons is provided in the pages of this creative study of the United States.

Forte, Imogene and Sandra Schurr. *The Cooperative Learning Guide and Planning Pak for Middle Grades.* Nashville, TN: Incentive Publications, 1992.

> This resource presents a collection of high-interest thematic units, thematic thinking skills projects, and thematic poster projects. Includes teacher's overviews, reference skills sharpeners, content mini-units, design-your-own units, and more.

Forte, Imogene and Sandra Schurr. *The Definitive Middle School Guide.* Nashville, TN: Incentive Publications, 1993.

> Each of seven modules includes an overview, glossary, findings from the published literature, informational pages in a convenient "Top Ten" format, and "teacher activities" keyed to Bloom's Taxonomy. All are designed to facilitate interdisciplinary teaming and thematic instructional planning.

Forte, Imogene and Sandra Schurr. *Science Mind Stretchers.* Nashville, TN: Incentive Publications, 1987.

> Mind-stretching interdisciplinary activities for life, earth, and physical science. Each mini-unit consists of reproducible topical overview activity pages and two or more extending worksheets. All are designed to teach basic science concepts while developing vital reasoning skills and stimulating curiosity about the world of science.

Forte, Imogene and Sandra Schurr. *Tools, Treasures, and Measures.* Nashville, TN: Incentive Publications, 1994.

> The tools are lively, effective student activities and assignments created especially for middle graders. The treasures are valuable lists, lesson plans, and information sheets. The measures provide up-to-date assessment instruments, techniques, records, and reporting systems. Together, these tools, treasures, and measures form a significant collection of instructional materials and models for the middle grades instructor.

Frank, Marjorie. *If You're Trying To Teach Kids How To Write, You've Gotta Have This Book!* Nashville, TN: Incentive Publications, Inc., 1979.

> This how-to book describes understanding and working with the whole writing process and serves as an at-your-fingertips source of ideas for starting specific activities and a ready-when-you're-in-need manual for solving writing problems.

Frank, Marjorie. *Using Writing Portfolios To Enhance Instruction and Assessment.* Nashville, TN: Incentive Publications, Inc., 1994.

> This comprehensive guide defines the writing portfolio and covers designing the portfolio, portfolio management, guidelines for evaluation, and a host of creative portfolio activity ideas.

Frender, Gloria. *Learning To Learn.* Nashville, TN: Incentive Publications, Inc., 1990.

> Designed to help students learn how to learn more effectively, this book is filled with ideas, hints, methods, procedures, and resources that provide "hands-on" materials for study skills including note-taking, organizational skills, test-taking, memory skills, power reading, problem-solving, and time management.

Frender, Gloria. *Teaching for Learning Success.* Nashville, TN: Incentive Publications, Inc., 1994.

> This comprehensive manual has all the materials needed for cooperative learning, independent study, teaching to varied learning styles, organizing the classroom for successful management, unit and lesson plans, and accompanying reproducible student pages.

Index